THE TYNE &
WEAR METRO

Colin Alexander

AMBERLEY

Cover: Passing the Blue House foot crossing between East Boldon and Seaburn is an Airport to South Hylton train formed of refurbished Metrocars Nos 4068 and 4059, on 24 July 2014. (Alex Thorkildsen)

First published 2020

Amberley Publishing
The Hill, Stroud
Gloucestershire, GL5 4EP

www.amberley-books.com

Copyright © Colin Alexander, 2020

The right of Colin Alexander to be identified
as the Author of this work has been asserted in
accordance with the Copyrights, Designs and
Patents Act 1988.

ISBN 978 1 3981 0157 9 (print)
ISBN 978 1 3981 0158 6 (ebook)

British Library Cataloguing in Publication Data.
A catalogue record for this book is available from
the British Library.

Origination by Amberley Publishing.
Printed in the UK.

Contents

Introduction

The year 1829 saw a quiet revolution take place on the new railway between Liverpool and Manchester. A bright yellow machine named *Rocket*, built in Newcastle by the father and son team of George and Robert Stephenson, swept aside her competitors in the Rainhill Trials and created a sensation by reaching an unprecedented speed. The world changed, forever.

150 years later, another bright yellow transport revolution would change Tyneside forever.

August 2020 marked forty years since the opening of the first section of the Tyne & Wear Metro. In August 1980, my friends and I had a week-long Eastern Region Railrover (first class!), most of which we spent travelling behind 'Deltics' between King's Cross and Berwick. We took a short break from this to witness the last day of British Rail diesel operation from Tynemouth to Newcastle Central. This happened the day before the commencement of Metro services between Tynemouth and the new, purpose-built city centre underground station at Haymarket. It was a time of great pride and wonder on Tyneside, and people flocked to travel on the gleaming new system.

Several years later, when I lived in London and commuted by Underground every day, I was visiting my parents in Tynemouth one summer weekend. Boarding a standing-room-only Metro bound for the city centre to meet friends for a drink, I squeezed into a crowded vestibule among happy daytrippers returning home from a day at the seaside. There were babies in pushchairs, toddlers in arms, and children sitting on grandparents' knees. All of a sudden, as we accelerated through the cutting towards North Shields an elderly gentleman began singing 'Danny Boy' in a beautiful, deep voice. Others joined in and harmonised, or simply hummed along, and it seemed everyone was singing and smiling together. It is a moment in time that stayed with me, and it's one that I frequently revisited in my mind as I endured my daily Piccadilly line ordeal.

On another occasion, having returned to the north-east, I treated my retired neighbour to a ticket for a match at St James Park, and after his wife dropped us off at Shiremoor Metro station, I detected a look of child-like excitement on his face. When I pointed out that watching Newcastle United was not that thrilling, he explained to me that he had never been on the Metro before, and was looking forward to that experience! This took me by surprise, as our Metro was, by then, thirty years old and was very much a part of everyday life on the banks of the Tyne and the Wear. Clearly, though, it still held some magic.

We love our Metro, especially those of us who are old enough to remember what went before it, and I am particularly proud of the system, as my late father was involved in its development. An engineering draughtsman who had learned his trade at legendary Newcastle turbine manufacturer Parsons, he was unexpectedly made redundant about 1974 from the British Ship Research Association in Wallsend. There, in conjunction with Swan Hunter, he had worked on the engineering drawings for the massive Tyne-built 250,000-ton 'super-tankers' such as the *Esso Northumbria.*

This proud man's despair at redundancy quickly turned to joy when he started work at Cuthbert House in Newcastle for the fledgling Tyne & Wear Passenger Transport Executive, whose plans for a new, light rapid-transit system for Tyneside were in the early stages. Once the system was in operation, Dad relocated to an office at the depot in South Gosforth. His role was Technical Assistant in the Rolling Stock section, where his 'Dance of the Sugar Plum Draughtsman' was apparently a sight to behold!

During the preparation of this book, I was privileged to attend one of the regular reunions of almost thirty of my Dad's colleagues. It is, I think, a testimony to their sense of camaraderie, that twenty-six years after my father's retirement, so many of his former workmates are still in regular contact. Many of them kindly provided me with images and anecdotes for the book.

As a schoolboy railway enthusiast growing up in the 1970s, I was aware of the Metro systems of major world cities like London, New York, Paris, Moscow and Tokyo. It was highly exciting that Newcastle was to have its own 'underground', something which would have put a smile on the face of that great son of Tyneside, George Stephenson, who in the early nineteenth century predicted that trains would one day be powered by electricity.

It is, of course, entirely appropriate, that Britain's first fully integrated, fully inclusive light rapid-transit system should be built in the 'cradle of the railways'. In fact, today's Metro 'supertrams' pass within a mile of Killingworth Colliery, where Stephenson's first 'iron horses' steamed more than 200 years ago; and burrow underneath the factory he established, where he and his son, Robert, built their most famous locomotives.

A journey on the Metro can take us past open fields, terraces of Tyneside flats, tower blocks, leafy suburbs and sandy beaches. It can carry us to Roman forts, Saxon churches, mediaeval castles and ruined monasteries. Metro serves the UK's eleventh busiest airport, three universities, two of England's biggest football grounds and an international athletics venue. It is unique.

Continuing as it did the north-east's long tradition of pioneering and innovation, we are proud of our Metro, but I think that forty years on, many of the travelling public take it for granted.

The shape of things to come, 1975. Metro Test Centre, Middle Engine Lane, North Shields. Prototype Metro-Cammell Supertram/Metrocar No. 4001 shows off her original yellow and cream livery, complete with maroon bogies. (Brian Pearson)

On the occasion of its fortieth anniversary, it is time to celebrate its success and innovation, and look forward to its future.

I would like to acknowledge the various photographic contributors, especially friend and former colleague of my Dad, Graham Pearson; and Alex Thorkildsen for providing such a wealth of high-quality images. Huge thanks also to Scott Lowes, Paul Williams and David Dunn for their major contributions.

An enormous debt of gratitude is owed to David Thornton and the Reverend Joan Thornton for their hospitality and for allowing me access to some treasured documents. David was Rolling Stock Maintenance Engineer, initially at the Test Centre, and was another close colleague of my late father. He kindly acted as proof-reader, too.

I am grateful for the help and encouragement of several other former PTE colleagues of my Dad: Jim Davidson, Eddie Blackburn, Dick Bourne, Terry Matthews, Tony Warren and Stuart Little. I also received enormous help and support from Lynne Robinson, Public Affairs Manager at Nexus and her colleague, David Bayles, Communications Assistant.

Thank you also to the other individual photographers, who are credited in the captions.

Special thanks to Will Walker for recounting his personal experience, and many thanks to Daniel Wright for the use of his excellent 'The Beauty of Transport' blog. Finally, thank you to Keith McNally of the Stephenson Railway Museum for his help with some of the Metro Test Centre photographs, as well as Keith Nye and Iain Munro for their input.

I humbly dedicate this book to the memory of my father, John 'Jack' Alexander MBE, who loved railways, loved Tyneside and was so proud of the Metro system which he served.

1

Metro Prehistory

As could be expected in a region of such railway heritage, the Tyne & Wear Metro's network has a rich history, with some of its routes dating back to the 1830s. This heritage will be explored later in the book as we journey around the system, but what did the Metro replace?

Immediately before its opening in 1980, Tyneside's commuters were served by a fleet of British Rail diesel-mechanical multiple units (DMUs) dating from the late 1950s. They were quite reliable, with well-sprung seating, and if the driver left the cab partition blinds up, they offered an unrivalled forward view from the front seats. They were, however, slow to accelerate and their underfloor diesel engines rattled noisily. What is more, they made a loss of about £1.5 million per annum. In the late 1970s, I was travelling on a DMU through the soot-blackened Victorian tunnels under North Shields when, below the floor, its engine caught fire. The blaze was quickly extinguished, and we were on our way again.

When the DMUs took over Tyneside's suburban services in the 1960s, they were seen as a retrograde step, replacing as they did the popular, fast and comfortable electric trains. It was the pioneering North Eastern Railway reacting to competition from the growing tram network that introduced the 'Tyneside Electrics' as early as 1904. This was acknowledged to be Britain's first electric suburban railway.

Its successor, the LNER, replaced the wooden-bodied electric fleet in 1937 with modern articulated units in a bright two-tone livery, echoing the future Metro fleet. The trains were well-loved by the public, but by the 1960s the entire infrastructure was in need of replacement. It was decided, therefore, to de-electrify the lines and run DMUs instead.

In an attempt to revitalise the suburban network, BR's local publicity department came up with the 'Tynerail' and 'Tynerider' brands in the early 1970s. Some of the DMU vehicles were given colourful local names such as 'Cushy Butterfield', 'Harry Hotspur' and 'Bobby Shaftoe', which were applied as vinyl stickers. This, however, could not compensate for the increasingly shabby and unwelcoming condition of our local stations, many of which were unstaffed and, in some cases, dangerous. My father, who was not a big man, was hurt quite badly when he fell through the rotten timbers of the platform at Wallsend station in the early 1970s.

Car ownership, meanwhile, was on the rise, and commuters abandoned the North Tyne loop and South Shields branch, taking to their Cortinas and Marinas. I seem to remember Bob Ferris, (played by Rodney Bewes) in television's *Whatever Happened to the Likely Lads* and his aspirational wife, Thelma, favoured the Vauxhall Viva. Neither they nor their upwardly mobile neighbours in the Elm Lodge Estate would have dreamed of using the Tynerider trains, but they might have used the Metro!

It seems incredible now that the pedestrianised Northumberland Street in Newcastle city centre was the route of the A1 London to Edinburgh trunk road as late as 1975, when the Central Motorway cut a concrete swathe through leafy Jesmond. Every attempt to increase capacity on the roads, particularly the Tyne crossings, led to increased usage and further congestion. The Metro was designed to reverse that trend and take passenger traffic from the roads.

Newcastle Central station, forty-three years before Metro services began. This was the inaugural run on the North Tyne loop of the new 1937 stock, complete with the smartly attired driver standing proudly alongside. In a parallel with the Tyne & Wear Metrocars the twin units were articulated in the centre and carried a bright two-tone livery. One of the original Edwardian wooden-bodied electric trains is on the right. (DR Dunn collection)

Fast forward just over thirty years to about 1970, and the electric third rail has been lifted. This classic view of Newcastle Central taken from the Norman Castle Keep shows all of the east end bay platforms as a Metro-Cammell DMU sets off for the coast. With Metro services being routed underground, these bays became redundant and are now a car park. Always regarded as inferior to their electric predecessors, the DMUs kept services going until the next Metro-Cammell product arrived on Tyneside. (Jack Alexander MBE)

2

Metro Conception

In 1969, the Tyneside Passenger Transport Authority was formed and in 1971, its publication 'Rapid Transit for Tyneside' detailed the rationale for a light rapid-transit Metro system. It identified that the city and its suburbs needed movement to prosper, and that the motor car was necessary. The exponential increase in car ownership of the 1960s and 1970s, however, was increasing congestion and pollution, as well as hindering the movement of buses.

It was acknowledged that a light rapid-transit network could form the speedy, traffic-free core of an integrated public transport system to relieve the traffic jams that snarled up the Tyne crossings on a daily basis. Being electric, it would be quiet and with zero exhaust emissions, and by making use of the existing suburban rail network, it would minimise urban blight and land acquisition. However, it had to be capable of future extension.

Perhaps if a Tyne & Wear Metro system was being considered now, it would resemble the later street trams of Manchester, Sheffield and several other British cities. Back in the 1970s though, only a decade or so after the last traditional tramways had been lifted, perhaps Britain was not ready for trams, hence the bold decision to burrow beneath the city centre. The *Financial Times* described the Metro concept at the time as an "amalgam of all that looks best about lightweight rapid transit systems in other European countries".

A far-reaching 1971 document entitled 'The Transport Plan for the 1980s' promised not only to provide better public transport for Tyneside, but also to stimulate inner-city redevelopment in places like Gateshead and Byker, and in turn, the wider local economy. The *Financial Times* described it as a "lynchpin in the conurbation's regeneration, as a prime instrument for stemming the inner areas' loss of population and jobs."

1973's 'Plan for the People' recognised that car ownership was on the increase and while many in government questioned the need for public transport at all, its necessity was acknowledged for the elderly, children and those without their own cars. With admirable

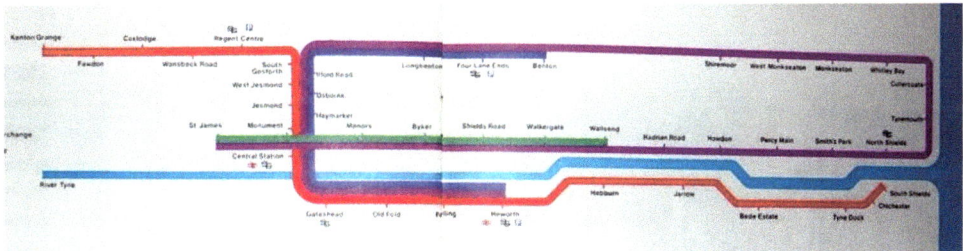

An early iteration of the Metro route map, dating from 1971. Osborne, Kenton Grange and Old Fold would become West Jesmond, Bank Foot and Gateshead Stadium, respectively. (Colin Alexander collection)

foresight, this document announced that road building alone was not the answer. European research revealed that a well-planned blend of public and private transport enhanced the communities they served.

After several alternatives were considered, including a thankfully aborted network of urban motorways, the PTE's 'Tyneside Metropolitan Railway Bill' successfully passed through Parliament, and Royal Assent was received in July 1973.

In 1974, the Metropolitan County of Tyne and Wear was created by grafting the populous south-east corner of Northumberland to the north-east corner of County Durham. It also encompassed the historic City of Newcastle-upon-Tyne. The new county had a population of over 1 million. The leader of the new county council, Michael Campbell, persuaded the government to back our Metro against a context of scarce public funds. The *Financial Times* said, "The survival of this project thus far ... probably owes as much to the stamina and enthusiasm of its progenitors as to the ingenuity of their design."

Construction of what would become Britain's largest urban transport project of the twentieth century commenced for real in 1974 at Jesmond.

Meet Your Metro was a glossy A4 booklet published by the Tyne & Wear Passenger Transport Executive in 1977 to whet the public appetite for the scheme. It began, "Metro and a new-style bus route network have been designed to bring a vast improvement to public transport in Tyne & Wear." It went on "Metro and bus services will together form an integrated transport system to open up the whole area to an extent not previously possible ... "

A collection of some of the publicity material that was printed before and after the opening. There is a leaflet introducing the Test Centre, and 'Meet Your Metro', which was a glossy colour brochure to whet the public appetite. Alongside is 'Horse Tram to Metro', which plundered the archives and showed how public transport had evolved in Tyne and Wear. At the bottom is a beautiful double-page spread from the brochure commemorating the Royal opening in November 1981. (Colin Alexander, with thanks to David Thornton)

Tyneside would be "the first area in the United Kingdom to have a fully integrated public transport system made up of Metro and bus services". Sadly, this innovative integration of bus, Metro and ferry would be short-lived, due to the deregulation of buses introduced by the Thatcher government in 1986.

A total of forty-two stations was initially planned, linking towns on both banks of the Tyne between Newcastle and the coast, as well as a branch north west to Bank Foot in the direction of the airport. The plan was for three main types of station; city centre underground stations, bus interchanges, and simple Metro halts. All were designed to be easy to clean and maintain, with vandal-proof panelling.

It was then decided to retain much of the fabric of several Victorian stations, which added much character and variety. New stations were built where none stood previously, to serve recent housing and retail developments, and the route deviated from its predecessors in key locations such as Gateshead and Byker, to better serve those centres.

Future extensions were also taken into consideration in the early planning stages, and some of these have since come to fruition.

Metro was the first British transport network to embrace truly inclusive design, providing step-free access at all stations from street level to train for wheelchair users, and was a smoke-free zone from the outset. Later, the seating layout of the trains was altered to further increase capacity for wheelchairs and pushchairs, as well as creating extra luggage room for airport-bound passengers.

Under the Tyne & Wear PTE, the Metro was integrated with the metropolitan county's bus services, the British Rail Newcastle–Sunderland line and the Shields Ferry, with through ticketing known as 'Transfares'. The vibrant colour scheme of cadmium yellow and white with its distinctive Tyne & Wear PTE logo, already carried by PTE buses and the ferries, was extended to the Metrocars. The livery was derived from the traditional yellow and cream Newcastle Corporation bus colours, as replicated on the Test Centre prototypes. Bus interchanges were built at strategic locations such as Four Lane Ends, Gateshead, Heworth and Regent Centre.

The stations were designed by local architects Ainsworth Spark and Faulkner Brown and featured innovative noise-reducing trough-shaped ceilings. They were unstaffed, with automatic ticket vending machines and ticket-operated barriers throughout. The latter were subsequently removed following safety concerns, in fact a friend of my brother, then aged seven years old, became trapped in one of the barriers, and his account of that terrifying incident is below. A different type of barrier was subsequently installed, but only at the busiest stations. The whole network is controlled from the Metro Control Room at South Gosforth from which a CCTV system keeps a watchful eye, supported by roving ticket inspectors.

The principal underground stations boasted extra-large Calvert slab-serif lettering, as seen at Monument in 2019. (Colin Alexander)

One of Metro's most distinctive features is its graphic design. Typographer Margaret Calvert, who in the late 1950s and early 1960s worked with Jock Kinneir to bring order and a new identity to Britain's road signs, was commissioned to design a new typeface. Daniel Wright, in his blog 'The Beauty of Transport', says,

> If you want my nomination for Britain's most literate public transport network branding, I'd put forward Tyne and Wear's without hesitation. Eschewing the pictures, pictograms, graphics and icons relied upon by many other public transport networks, Tyne and Wear's instead puts typography at its heart". He goes on to say that "The typeface is a slab-serif, which Calvert considered was appropriate to the architectural quality of Newcastle itself... a perfect fit with Newcastle and the wider area served by the Metro."

The most eye-catching application of Calvert's typeface is on the enamelled panels of the subterranean stations such as Monument where the name is emblazoned in giant blue letters along the platforms. St James is in black, Manors in red, and so on. These are gradually being replaced by a newer, stylish monochrome version in the same font.

Daniel Wright again,

> The Calvert typeface, and in particular the black M on a yellow background, became as locally distinctive as the London Underground roundel is to Londoners. Outside Metro stations, you'll find illuminated totems with a yellow box at the top, each vertical side displaying a Calvert "M". The instant and enduring popularity of the Metro with local people and visitors cemented a link between the colour yellow, Calvert lettering, and decent local transport.

The "M" would also eventually supplant the Tyne & Wear PTE logo on the Metrocar fleet.

In 1996, Tyne & Wear PTE became Nexus, following which the Metro's visual identity suffered some years of inconsistency. In 2009, as part of Nexus's "Metro – All Change" programme, Newcastle design firm Gardiner Richardson overhauled Metro's branding, stripping it back

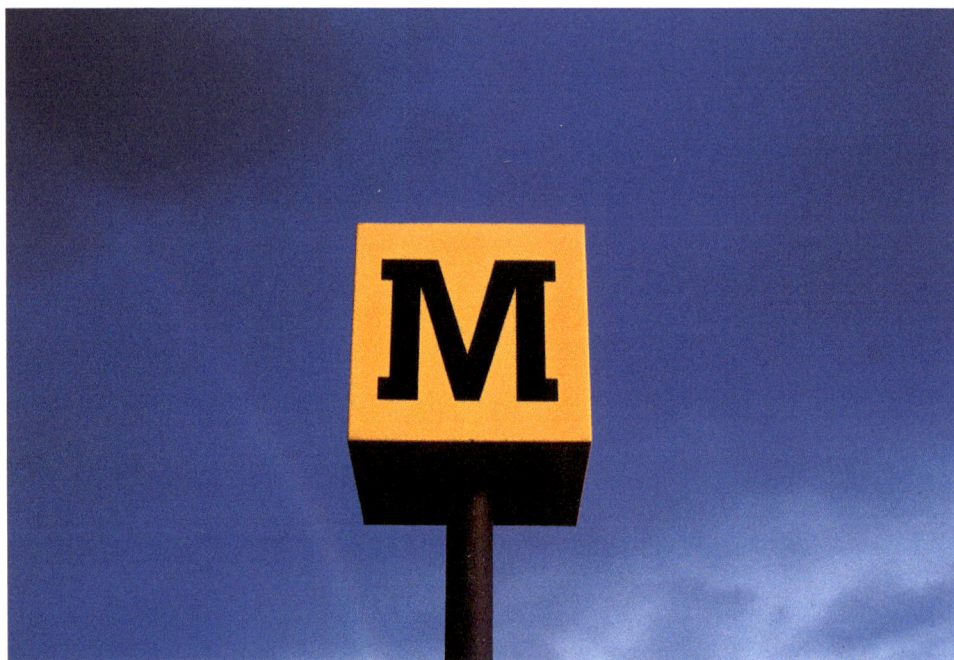

The iconic Metro 'M', designed by Margaret Calvert, as seen outside Whitley Bay station in November 1984. (Paul Williams)

This is the black and white colour scheme, as featured in the football-related theme at St James station. (Colin Alexander)

to its most basic elements, namely the colour yellow and the Calvert typeface. Pretty much everything else would be monochrome, making the yellow stand out. As Daniel Wright says, it sounds drab, but it is quite brilliant, putting Calvert's iconic typeface and Metro's traditional yellow centre stage, but presented in a clean and crisp manner with a visual integrity that meets modern expectations.

The Metro map is another familiar sight to the commuters of Tyne & Wear, and like most of the world's public transport maps it traces its lineage back to Harry Beck's pre-war London Underground map. It was Beck who revolutionised transport mapping, ignoring geographical scale, removing unnecessary clutter and straightening lines. Diagrammatic rather than cartographical, the Metro map's colour-coding with horizontal, diagonal and vertical lines is pure Harry Beck. Just as the Thames is the only non-railway feature on the 'tube' map, the same is true of the Tyne and the Wear on ours.

Complementing the graphical harmony of the Metro is its collection of art installations, which number more than fifty, some of which are described as we explore the network, later. "Art on public transport can make the difference between a journey being an endurance test or a pleasure", according to Andrew Knight, Public Art Consultant for Nexus.

3

Metro Testing

In 2020, Middle Engine Lane, on the north-western fringe of North Shields, is a busy road carrying traffic to and from surrounding retail parks and businesses. In the early 1970s, however, it was a quiet backwater, a narrow road between featureless, scruffy fields and stunted trees. It took its name from a long-gone winding-engine house on one of the many inclined waggonways which crossed it on their way from the Northumberland coalfield to the staithes on the Tyne. It would soon become a hive of activity with the construction of the Metro Test Centre, financed by a government Research & Development Grant with support from Tyne & Wear County Council. Construction began in November 1974 and the first train ran in June 1975.

It was intended principally as a test facility for the two prototype Tyne & Wear Metrocars, built by Metropolitan-Cammell in Birmingham. It was also a venue where that firm and other

Early days at the Test Centre, *c.* 1975, looking south across Middle Engine Lane. The level crossing is temporarily protected by portable traffic lights. The fields beyond the road are now completely obliterated by car dealerships and the Silverlink retail park. (Graham Pearson)

An auspicious occasion in 1975 as the first Supertram or Metrocar, No. 4001, makes her debut on Tyneside. She is being craned onto the rails at the Test Centre, following delivery from Metro-Cammell in Birmingham. Note that some of the lower body-side panels have been removed for access to the lifting points. (Graham Pearson)

associated manufacturers could showcase their products to a global market. Indeed, transport operators and light rapid-transit engineers from every continent visited the centre during its operation.

The only train to be tested there, other than the Tyne & Wear twins, was a Metro-Cammell product destined for Hong Kong's new mass transit system, in early 1978. My Dad took me to the test centre more than once, and as well as getting to drive Nos 4001 and 4002 (under close supervision), I am one of the few people to have travelled on the Hong Kong Metro in North Shields!

My (much) younger brother, who could only have been aged about four or five years old at the time, was also allowed to drive one of the prototype Metrocars under even closer supervision. Weren't we lucky boys to have such a big train set to play with?

More importantly than its role as a global showcase, the Test Centre also served as a massive publicity exercise for the new system. Surprisingly, there had been a lot of public suspicion about the new system, and in some instances opposition to it. This was borne of a fear that its cost would be met from increases in rates, and also due to the inevitable disruption in the city centre during excavation work. This was countered by inviting school parties and Women's Institute groups to the Test Centre for talks and a free ride up and down the line. They would naturally spread the word about this wonderful, clean, new mode of transport, and the public was, of course, won over.

Incidentally, another turning point in public opinion was when the Newcastle Journal, having previously been hostile, postulated that property prices would increase in areas served by Metro. Remarkably, over 11,000 visitors were received during the short lifetime of this unique facility.

Another publicity exercise was the full-size wooden mock-up of a Metro train and underground platform, which was open to the public in Melbourne Street in Newcastle.

Far East meets north-east in North Shields. The first Metro-Cammell cars for the new Hong Kong Metro are seen on test at Middle Engine Lane in February 1978. (Mike Arkley)

The Test Centre was based around a purpose-built car-shed and workshop, with an inspection pit and lifting jacks. It had its own offices, control room and electrical substation providing the 2.4 km of track with 1500v DC overhead power. The rails were laid on the redundant track-beds of sections of the Backworth Colliery Railway and the Seatonburn Waggonway of 1826, which once carried Northumberland coal to the Tyne for shipping.

The test track extended north of Middle Engine Lane, which it traversed by means of an automatic level crossing, into a short tunnel through an artificial hill in a field, through a passing loop with minimum-radius reverse curves and terminated at West Allotment. The level crossing, at the recommendation of the Railway Inspectorate, was protected by warning lights only to prove that a crossing without barriers could work. It would also serve to educate motorists who would have to get used to such crossings on the future Metro system.

The tunnel was used for a practice evacuation, using PTE staff as 'passengers', in which it was proven that there would be sufficient space in the tunnels for longitudinal walkways for use in emergencies, therefore obviating the need for the end doors that were fitted to the prototype Metrocars.

To the south of the depot the test track ran as far as the A1058 Coast Road, where it ended at the foot of a 1 in 25 gradient. Collectively, the features of the test track were designed to simulate the full range of potential operating conditions. There was even a prototype ticket machine trialled there, even though no tickets would ever be sold!

The two prototype cars had electrical equipment supplied by GEC and fabricated steel bogies from German firm Düwag. It was a wise move to opt for tried-and-tested continental equipment, for the near-contemporary Bay Area Rapid Transit (BART) system in San Francisco employed untried brand-new technology, which caused an array of teething troubles. David Thornton, then in charge of the Metro Test Centre, was quoted in the *Financial Times* as saying "there

The Hunslet diesel shunter, works No. 4264 of 1952, is in charge of the wiring train beside the artificial tunnel between Middle Engine Lane and West Allotment. The locomotive had previously been employed at Portsmouth Dockyard. (Graham Pearson)

Inside the Test Centre's purpose-built depot, the Hunslet diesel shares one of the roads with the second prototype Metrocar, No. 4002. The Tyne & Wear PTE logo is prominent on both vehicles. (Graham Pearson)

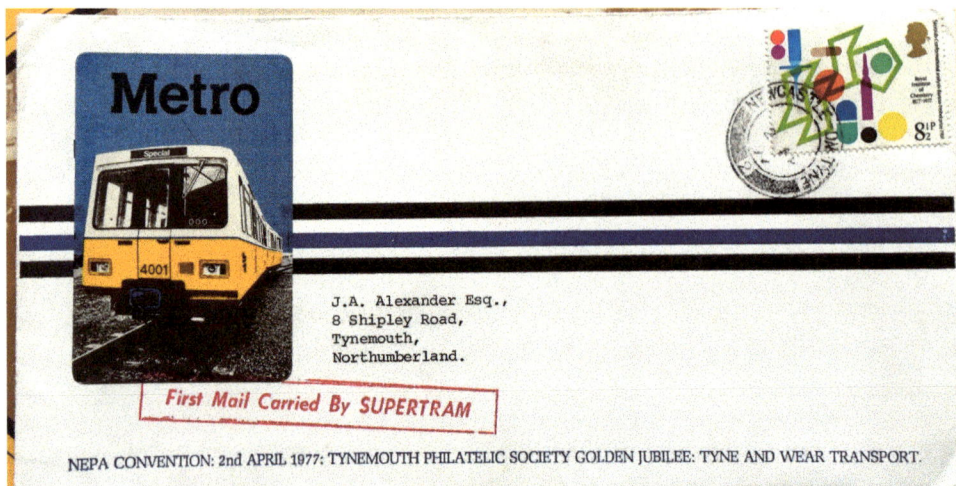

This Royal Mail first-day cover, dating from 1977, was sent to my father and proclaims itself to be the first mail carried by Supertram, on the Test Track. (Colin Alexander)

just wasn't time for anything new-fangled. We need a system which will be reliable as soon as it comes into use."

Dick Bourne, another colleague of my father, relates a tale from the Test Centre:

Two drivers, John Peffers and George Jackson, were appointed from existing PTE staff, and this stalwart pair were engaged in driving the prototype Metrocars up and down the test track to accumulate mileage. One day, George was the source of a vital safety observation. Whilst engaged in some testing activity, we were in the middle of the moving train, huddled over some instrumentation. George's voice came from behind us "Goin' OK is it, lads?"

This was worrying, as George was the driver. But, how?

As with all trains, the controls embodied a Driver's Safety Device (DSD) *(Author's note - often known as the 'deadman's handle)* which would stop the train automatically should the driver become incapacitated. George, how come we're still moving? "I'll show you!", came the cheery reply. George demonstrated that the T-shaped controller handle that included the DSD could be held down by a packet of twenty cigarettes wedged under the cab light switch on the wall. The design was subsequently modified!

The bodies and roofs of the Tyneside vehicles, dubbed 'Supertrams', were aluminium with front ends of glass-fibre-reinforced polymer. Each car consisted of two body sections articulated on the unpowered, centre bogie; with the two outer bogies each carrying a longitudinal traction motor driving two output shafts, rated at 187kw each. The Metrocar was designed for quiet operation, with fast acceleration and a maximum speed of 80 km/h. As well as the ability to get away from stations rapidly, the cars could stop like no train I had ever been on before, with their rheostatic and disc brakes as well as large magnetic emergency track brakes.

Each articulated 'twin' weighed 39 tonnes, measuring 27.8 metres in length and with a seating capacity of eighty-four. Incidentally, from the outset, the Tyne & Wear Metro adopted the metric system of measurement, with its 80 km/h speed limit and 1435 mm track gauge.

Testing of Nos 4001 and 4002 began at Middle Engine Lane in 1975. One problem that became apparent was wear to wheel flanges and rails on sharp curves. This resulted in the installation of automatic rail-greasers and the use of manganese-steel rails at locations such as Jesmond, where curvature is severe.

No. 4002 is seen in August 1978 at the temporary platform just south of the Test Centre depot. The prototypes had door operating mechanisms from Kiekert in Germany. It is thought that the unpainted doors on No. 4002 were supplied by British firm Westinghouse, for comparison. (Neil Sinclair)

Raised on the Test Centre depot's jacks, No. 4002 receives some attention to one of her powered bogies. (Jack Alexander MBE)

It is ironic that the depot built as part of the test facility for the Tyne & Wear Metro now houses the only surviving vehicle from the original North Eastern Railway 1904 electric car fleet. Beautifully restored motor parcel van No. 3267 is displayed in the fascinating Stephenson Railway Museum on Middle Engine Lane. (Colin Alexander)

As well as the Metrocars, the Test Centre boasted a Hunslet 0-4-0 diesel shunter, which, with its flat wagons was used during the installation of the overhead catenary.

Following the opening of the Metro system proper, the Test Centre would eventually become the headquarters of the Stephenson Railway Museum, and the operating base for the North Tyneside Steam Railway. This is the railway section of Tyne & Wear Museums.

The museum houses a fascinating collection of exhibits, including *Billy*, the third oldest locomotive in existence in the world. She is also the oldest surviving Stephenson engine, built at nearby Killingworth in 1816. Appropriately, the old Test Centre is home to the only survivor from the original North Tyneside electric multiple unit fleet, beautifully restored North Eastern Railway motor parcels van No. 3267, dating from 1904.

There is also the only working example of motive power from Tyneside's other historic electric railway, the Harton Electric Railway, which carried coal to staithes at South Shields. Locomotive E4 was built by Siemens in 1909 and is fully restored. The museum's Metro heritage is represented by a full-size mock-up of a Metrocar cab.

4

Metro Construction

Much of the Metro construction work consisted of upgrading, resignalling and electrifying the existing 'heavy rail' routes around the North Tyneside loop and later along the South Shields branch.

According to Jim Davidson, who was Project Director and responsible for liaison between the PTE and the Railway Inspectorate, much of the permanent way inherited from British Railways was very neglected. Antiquated 'bullhead' rail was laid on rotten sleepers that were carried on unstable embankments. After five years of negotiations, BR agreed to a £16 million payment to Tyne & Wear PTE under the euphemistic heading of 'deferred maintenance'.

At the insistence of the erstwhile Tyne & Wear County Council, the Metro 'corridor' was to be screened from residential streets by the planting of trees. This would prove costly over time as maturing roots disturbed embankments, branches conflicted with overhead power lines and of course, as the trees matured, every autumn brought wheel adhesion problems with damp, fallen leaves on rails.

The section of the North Tyne loop between Manors and West Monkseaton (via Benton) closed to BR trains in 1978 to allow the conversion process to begin. This was followed by West Monkseaton to Tynemouth, and when Metro services began along this route from Tynemouth to Haymarket in 1980, the remaining stretch of North Tyne loop via Wallsend closed to BR services for its conversion. The closure of the South Shields BR line followed in 1981. As a temporary expedient, during construction work on these routes, Metro-link bus services were provided, stopping only at the former railway stations.

Most of the Metro stations were new and purpose-built, with a distinctive house-style, whether underground or on the surface. Happily, several of the original stations were retained and refurbished, adding a lot of character and interest to the system.

Work began in the city centre in 1972, when an exploratory borehole was drilled at the junction of Grainger Street and Market Street. Tunnelling work commenced properly in 1974, before the first prototype Metrocar had arrived at Middle Engine Lane. The new tunnels would form part of the 6.4 km of underground railway being excavated through the boulder clay of Newcastle and the ancient colliery workings of Gateshead. This latter obstacle caused some difficulty, where a honeycomb of exhausted mediaeval coal seams had to be filled and stabilised. Gateshead's new station was effectively a box constructed inside an old quarry. Not that tunnelling in Newcastle's boulder clay was straightforward. Due to subterranean burns (streams), especially between Monument and Central Station, the clay had to be temporarily artificially frozen in order for tunnel boring to take place.

The geological differences north and south of the river account for the different tunnelling methods employed. Newcastle has circular tunnels of 4.75 m diameter while Gateshead's have vertical sides and a width of 5 metres.

There was, unavoidably, some major disruption during tunnelling work under the city centre. Three notable structures on the surface required major work to prevent damage while work progressed beneath them. The foundations of Grey's Monument form a circular feature in the

As early as March 1972, the first exploratory work began in the city centre. This was the borehole site on Grainger Street, looking along Market Street towards the Theatre Royal. Close inspection of the sign reveals an accurate map of the central Metro zone as it would later appear, under the heading 'Tyneside Transit'. (Photograph courtesy of Nexus)

Jesmond was the point at which the first Metro services went underground. The station is just below surface level and was a focus for the earliest mid-1970s excavations. Newcastle Civic Centre and Jesmond Parish Church are in the background. (Graham Pearson)

Above: A fascinating view underneath Blackett Street showing the concrete and steel reinforcements forming the strengthened foundations of Grey's Monument. This circular structure is a prominent feature in the subterranean ticket concourse. (Photograph courtesy of Nexus)

Right: Blackett Street on 23 August 1978, less than two years before services would commence between Tynemouth and Haymarket, and excavations at the Monument were at an advanced stage. (Photograph courtesy of Nexus)

subterranean ticket concourse of Monument station; while the iconic portico of Newcastle Central station and, over the river, the side of Gateshead's BR diesel depot, had to be partly dismantled and rebuilt.

Apart from the underground sections, there were several other substantial engineering accomplishments during Metro's construction. Among them is the 165-metre-long Bridge N.106, 25 metres above the Tyne and built by Cleveland Bridge & Engineering Co., who had previously been responsible for the bridge at Ballachulish in Scotland, on which design it is based. The elegant concrete Byker Viaduct carries Metro over the Ouseburn Valley and into Byker station. The bridge is 820 metres long and 30 metres high and was built outwards from both sides of the valley simultaneously. It was said that when the two sections met in the middle, there was a misalignment of several inches. This was obviously remedied!

Another impressive statistic is that during the busiest stages of Metro construction, over 7,000 workers were employed.

The North Eastern Railway's former New Bridge Street goods yard, between Manors and Jesmond, was used by the PTE as a base for works trains. A BR Class 37 is seen here in the late 1970s, delivering a rake of bogie flat wagons for use in Metro construction. (Graham Pearson)

In a location which is almost unrecognisable now, two 0-4-0 diesel-mechanical shunters used during Metro construction stand at New Bridge Street, in 1986. Nearest is Hunslet No. 4212 of 1950, obtained from NEI-Parsons at nearby Heaton. The other is the locomotive previously used on the Metro test track at Middle Engine Lane. (Gordon Edgar)

Sometime in the late 1970s, a BR Class 31 diesel-electric locomotive and a steam crane are involved in track-laying work on the Bank Foot branch, with the Regent Centre complex in the background. This would become an important Metro-bus interchange. (Graham Pearson)

BR's English Electric Class 37 diesels were regular visitors to the Callerton line and the Rowntrees factory at Fawdon, which, from 1981, meant sharing the Bank Foot branch with Metrocars. In this photograph, however, No. 37045 is engaged in construction work at Fawdon, *c.* 1978. (Keith Brown)

The northern approach to bridge N.106 is freshly ballasted and awaits the laying of the permanent way. BR's Gateshead engine shed, soon to be swept away completely, is opposite. (Graham Pearson)

The twin tunnel bores below Newcastle Central station. Bridge N.106 is behind the photographer. (Graham Pearson)

By 28 March 1980, the underground concourse and access stairs at Monument were taking shape. There are a total of four exits from the underground station here, including a lift for step-free access from Metro trains into Eldon Square shopping centre, part of which is visible left of the base of Grey's Monument. The station would open to the public in November 1981. (Photograph courtesy of Nexus)

Following cessation of BR services on the line from Newcastle to Tynemouth via Wallsend in August 1980, conversion work began ready for its November 1982 Metro opening. The platforms of Wallsend's new station are seen here under construction. A works train can be seen in the distance, marked by the blazing lights of one of the 'WL' diesels. (Graham Pearson)

Seen from the west side of the Ouseburn valley on 23 December 2019, the graceful curvature of Byker viaduct can be appreciated. (Colin Alexander)

5

Metro Opening, Operation and Development

By 1979, while civil engineering work continued, delivery of the main fleet of Metrocars was complete, having been hauled by rail from Metro-Cammell at Washwood Heath in Birmingham to South Gosforth. Brand-new No. 4077 stopped off at York en route for temporary display in the National Railway Museum, alongside iconic exhibits such as the world's fastest steam locomotive, Sir Nigel Gresley's LNER Class A4 No. 4468 *Mallard*. No. 4077 was one of the eighty-eight production-series Metrocars.

This is the rare sight of three Metrocars coupled together on one of the delivery runs from Metro-Cammell in Birmingham to South Gosforth depot, *c.* 1978. They were probably being hauled by a Class 37 diesel and are threading their way over the crossover towards a snowy BR Manors station. The photograph was taken from the windows of Cuthbert House, which housed the PTE offices at the time. (Graham Pearson)

Another delivery run from Metro-Cammell reaches journey's end. A BR Class 25 diesel with a single Metrocar, two barrier wagons and a brake van, is seen arriving at South Gosforth depot. (Graham Pearson)

A general view of South Gosforth depot during that transitional period when the site was shared by BR and the PTE. Brand-new Metrocars gleam amid the drab 'monastral blue' livery of BR stock, c. 1978. The two-storey building on the left contained the drawing office where my father worked, and reportedly performed the 'Dance of the Sugar Plum Draughtsman'! (Graham Pearson)

During the BR/PTE dual occupancy of South Gosforth depot, one could make interesting comparisons between 'heavy rail' vehicles and the new Supertrams. In mid-August 1979, BR 'Deltic' No. 55010 *The King's Own Scottish Borderer* made a rare visit to the depot to use the wheel turning lathe. The difference in height between her and the Metrocars is noticeable. (Jack Alexander MBE)

The order was originally for as many as 100 units, allowing the flexibility to operate longer trains, and in fact the platforms were originally designed with this in mind. Some of the underground platforms were actually built that way, but the actual usable lengths today are nearly all for two to two-and-a-half cars' length. The rest of the platform is hidden behind a "false" headwall and in many cases has been used as a place to hide equipment of various kinds.

The production Supertrams differed slightly from the two prototypes, most visibly in the omission of the doors on the front ends, and with different head/tail-light clusters and door-operating buttons. Another modification made to the design of the production series, compared to the prototypes, was the addition of external side doors to the cabs. On Nos 4001 and 4002 as originally built, the only cab doors were internal. In 1987, the prototype twins were modified to conform, and joined the main fleet.

In 1977, five 0-6-0 diesel-electric 'works' locomotives were ordered from Brush in Loughborough, numbered WL1–WL5. They were powered by Rolls-Royce engines, and they would prove invaluable on engineering trains during construction. It was recognised that the use of diesel locomotives in the tunnels would require special measures, and when delivered they were fitted with exhaust scrubbers similar to those fitted to diesel locos for coal mines. The device was basically a tank of water through which the exhaust bubbled to remove sulphurous content. The diesels were replaced in 1988 by three small battery-electric locomotives built by Hunslet of Leeds, augmented by some self-propelled convertible road-rail vehicles.

A special Metro train ran from Haymarket to Tynemouth on 7 August 1980, conveying staff and invited guests.

Three days later, on 10 August 1980, without fanfare, the last DMU rattled its way from Tynemouth to Newcastle Central and the following day was, to quote one of my favourite tunes of the time, by The Specials, the dawning of a new era.

It was on Monday, 11 August 1980 that regular services began operating from Haymarket to Tynemouth, serving intermediate stops at Jesmond, West Jesmond, Ilford Road, South Gosforth, Longbenton, Four Lane Ends, Benton, Shiremoor, West Monkseaton, Monkseaton, Whitley Bay

Between the end of BR services and the commencement of Metro operation, the PTE provided a regular bus service from station to station while conversion work was carried out. This is Leyland Atlantean No. 353 outside Tynemouth station on the R5 service to Central station via Wallsend, sometime in late 1980. In recent times, the original glazed awning outside the station entrance has been restored. (Ian J Robinson)

This photograph depicts a gauging trial taking place in the narrow cut-and-cover tunnels east of North Shields, which had been in use since 1847. A works locomotive is hauling twin Metrocars and has clearly stopped, as there is a member of staff standing on the roof of the train, checking clearances. (Graham Pearson)

Inside South Gosforth depot in November 1984 is one of the Brush-built diesel works locomotives, No. WL5. In 1991, all five were sold for use during the construction of the Channel Tunnel, and two survive in preservation. (Paul Williams)

One of the replacements for the Brush diesels, Hunslet battery-electric locomotive BL3 is flanked by refurbished Metrocars Nos 4041, 4057 and 4062 in the sunshine outside South Gosforth car sheds, 5 August 2018. (Scott Lowes)

Four days before public operations began, a special train ran from Haymarket to Tynemouth to mark the official opening on 7 August 1980. It carried only invited guests and is seen here at a wet South Gosforth station. (Graham Pearson)

By August 1980, the days of BR services at Tynemouth were numbered. As passengers disembark from a terminating DMU in the bay platform, having arrived from Newcastle Central via Wallsend, they cannot fail to notice the shiny Metrocar on test, below the footbridge. (Graham Pearson)

Another test train, headed by No. 4010, comes off the Byker Viaduct and approaches Byker station. Any comparison between the clean, new Metro infrastructure, and the shabbiness of what preceded it, will bring an appreciation of how momentous it all was. (Graham Pearson)

and Cullercoats. Metro had landed! To put the date into context, Mrs Thatcher had been Prime Minister for one year, Jimmy Carter was US President, and Abba topped the UK charts with *The Winner Takes It All*.

The system gradually opened in sections, with the branch from South Gosforth to Bank Foot, a route that had last seen passenger trains in 1929, opening in May 1981.

November 1981 saw the opening of the Underground route south from Haymarket through Monument and Central station, continuing across the Tyne into Gateshead and on to a new southern terminus at Heworth bus interchange.

This was an auspicious occasion in the history of the Metro, for it was marked by the visit of Her Majesty, Queen Elizabeth II and His Royal Highness, the Duke of Edinburgh, on Friday, 6 November 1981. The Royal Party and invited guests travelled on Metrocars Nos 4020 and 4007 from Monument to a specially erected platform at the north end of Bridge N.106. Following a delay due to a bomb scare, Her Majesty officially named the structure the Queen Elizabeth II Bridge. This continued a long tradition of Tyne crossings being opened by royalty, stretching back to 1849, when Queen Victoria opened the High Level Bridge. Meanwhile, the Metro Royal Train was delayed further because Prince Philip had strolled into the middle of the bridge to admire the view of the Tyne!

The train carrying the Queen and the Duke then crossed the river to Gateshead, where a plaque was unveiled, before continuing to Heworth. On arrival there, in an unrehearsed move, Prince Philip spoke to the driver of No. 4020, Jack Hall, and ended up sitting in his cab asking questions. The day concluded with a lavish reception in Newcastle Civic Centre.

The severe winter of 1981/2 caused much disruption to public transport everywhere, and the Metro was no exception. Although the Metrocars had been designed to operate in temperatures as low as $-10°$, the low-lying situation of South Gosforth car sheds and the prevailing south-westerly wind resulted in a recorded minimum of $-17°$! As a result, the pneumatic

Her Majesty Queen Elizabeth II
meets David Thornton, Traction
Maintenance Engineer, at Monument
station on 6 November 1981. This was
the date of the official Royal opening
of the Metro, although Tynemouth–
Haymarket services had been running
by then for fifteen months. David
Howard, General Manager of Tyne &
Wear Metro, is on the right, and partly
obscured by Her Majesty is Roger
Bagnall, Operating Superintendent.
(David Thornton collection)

On the same day, the Royal train led by
Metrocar No. 4020 stands between the
tunnels and the bridge, with the former
Stephenson locomotive works in the
background. The commemorative
headboard was one of several made, for
they were carried not only on this train
but also on two stand-by sets. The
headboards were later made into coffee
tables! (David Thornton collection)

The Royal party on the specially
erected platform alongside bridge
N.106, on the occasion of it being
officially named the Queen Elizabeth
II Bridge, 6 November 1981. The
tower blocks of Gateshead rise above
the engine sheds across the river, with
the infamous multi-storey car park
featured in the film *Get Carter*, partially
obscured by the Duke of Edinburgh.
(David Thornton collection)

Following the naming of the bridge, the Queen and Prince Philip rejoined their train and continued to Gateshead, where Her Majesty unveiled the plaque commemorating the official opening of the Tyne & Wear Metro and the sixth Tyne bridge. (David Thornton collection)

systems on the Metrocars froze, rendering brakes inoperable and trains immobile. They were subsequently modified to prevent a recurrence of the problem.

Metro did provide a service that winter when buses were unable to run. During my time working for BR's Signalling & Telecommunications Department I had to travel to a site in Birtley. Having got an early Metro from Tynemouth to Gateshead I found that no buses were running, so I had to walk 5 miles through the deep snow to report for duty!

By the following winter, in November 1982, the old North Tyne loop was complete, with the opening of the east–west line starting at St James, through Monument and Wallsend to Tynemouth.

By March 1984, all 55 km of the original planned network was operational, when the line from Heworth to South Shields opened.

Trains terminating at Heworth continued to the purpose-built sidings on the site of the old Pelaw station for the driver to change ends. An ex-colleague of my father related the story of a phone call received by South Gosforth Control Room from a frantic passenger who had somehow left his false teeth on a Metro that had terminated at Heworth. The driver of the train was radioed by control and when asked to search the train he paused and asked the controller if the teeth were a top-set or a bottom-set. Presumably this was in case there were multiple abandoned dentures on the train!

At this time there were four different line colours on the Metro route map. The yellow line ran from St James via Wallsend, Tynemouth, Benton and South Gosforth through to Heworth, and in doing so, passed beneath the centre of Newcastle twice. The green line began at Bank Foot, joining the yellow line at South Gosforth and continued beyond Heworth to South Shields. In addition, there were extra services running from Heworth to Benton, the red line on the map; and the blue line was St James to North Shields.

For most of each weekday, each colour line was served by a train every ten minutes, giving a service every five minutes on the east-west line in Newcastle City Centre and eighteen

Above: By 1987, a new generation of diesel multiple unit was being introduced on the national rail network. Some of those that were allocated to the remaining local services out of Newcastle were given a version of the PTE's yellow and white livery. New Class 143 'Pacer' No. 143020 is seen at South Gosforth depot alongside No. 4037. Is it a coincidence that the Metrocar is carrying reporting number 143 in the cab? (Graham Pearson)

Left: A southbound train speeds across the Queen Elizabeth II Bridge, and is about to enter the tunnel under Gateshead, in 1983. (Paul Williams)

trains per hour on the north–south line. Today's timetable just beats this on the north–south line, but only in peak hours, where there are four services (yellow line from St James to South Shields, green line from Airport to South Hylton, and peak services from Pelaw to Regent Centre and Pelaw to Monkseaton), each with a twelve-minute interval, providing twenty trains per hour. That such an intensity of service has been maintained for forty years with a fleet of no more than forty-five complete trains, despite major route extensions, is remarkable.

In September 1985, new intermediate stations were opened at Kingston Park and Pelaw, to be followed by Palmersville in March 1986.

In the first full year of Metro operation, over 60 million passenger journeys were made, demonstrating its effectiveness as the backbone of our new integrated transport network. This was highlighted in a government report in 1985. An interesting comparison of passenger figures at Benton and Tynemouth show that in 1911, in the early days of North Eastern Railway electric trains, the two stations generated 177,000 and 356,000 passenger journeys respectively. In 1995, Metro journeys from those two stations numbered 348,000 and 583,000. Even these latter figures were down, though, on Metro's mid-1980s peak.

A typical underground scene in the early days of Metro operation. This is Haymarket station in November 1984, showing the clean, modern appearance and bright colour scheme. (Paul Williams)

With the city's skyline as a backdrop this is Byker, looking west in October 1983, as a set led by No. 4018 comes off the viaduct into the station, and No. 4089 awaits departure for St James. (Paul Williams)

The 2011 Census showed that the proportion of people using Metro exceeded the national figure for commuting by train. In addition, the percentage of people commuting in Tyne & Wear by car is the UK's lowest outside London, which is largely down to Metro usage.

1989 saw the 150th anniversary of two of the Metro's predecessors, the Newcastle & North Shields Railway and the Brandling Junction Railway. Accordingly, Metrocars Nos 4051 and 4044 were turned out in N&NSR claret and BJR yellow liveries, respectively. Meanwhile the Metro fleet's iconic yellow and white livery gradually gave way to a new scheme, with the vehicles painted either blue, red or green, relieved by yellow doors and ends. Many of the Metrocars also carried advertising liveries from time to time.

At least eight examples of the Metrocar fleet had nameplates fitted to them, commemorating influential local people. Naturally, George and Robert Stephenson were given that accolade. Then there were Harry Cowans and Michael Campbell, two local politicians who were instrumental in pushing Metro through in its early stages; the eighteenth century Northumbrian engraver Thomas Bewick, Tyne & Wear PTE Chairman Danny Marshall; South Shields author Dame Catherine Cookson; and, last but not least, women's suffrage campaigner, MP and Jarrow March champion, Ellen Wilkinson.

It wasn't just the Test Centre that played host to visitors. On 17 September 1989, an open day was held at South Gosforth depot. A temporary platform was erected at the rear of the site, where prototype Metrocar No. 4002 has stopped with the shuttle service bringing visitors to the event. Notice the new light clusters on the front of the train, replacing the originals fitted to Nos 4001 and 4002. (Richard Vogel)

One of the named Metrocars was No. 4078 *Ellen Wilkinson*, commemorating the Labour MP for Jarrow who supported the 1936 marchers. (Elizabeth Tangora)

On 22 March 1983 at Brunton Lane, later the site of Kingston Park station, the driver of Tyne & Wear PTE Atlantean bus No. 220 drove onto the level crossing just as a Metro service comprising cars Nos 4083 and 4074 was approaching. Fortunately, the bus driver was its only occupant. Several passengers were on the train, however, and sustained minor injuries. The stricken bus is seen here being towed from the scene. (Colin Alexander)

In an all-yellow-and-white line up outside South Gosforth car sheds, Metrocar No. 4063 is the odd one out, showing off her newly applied Calvert 'M' that would replace the Tyne & Wear PTE logo on all of the trains. (Graham Pearson)

The Tyne & Wear Metro finally reached the Wear in 2002. Having emerged from the tunnels under Sunderland, prototype Supertram No. 4002 heads north across the Wearmouth Bridge and prepares to stop at St Peters station on the other side. The roof of the Stadium of Light can be discerned above the Metrocar. (D. R. Dunn collection)

The next major development was in November 1991 when the Bank Foot line was extended to Newcastle International Airport, providing Britain's fastest public transport link between a city centre and its airport, taking just twenty-three minutes. Part of this scheme was the provision of Callerton Parkway station for park-and-ride purposes.

For the first twenty-two years of Metro operation, the folk of Wearside must have questioned the name 'Tyne & Wear Metro', as it served exclusively those areas of population centred around the Tyne. A further investment of £100 million meant that Wearside would be included at last, with conversion of the existing Network Rail line from Pelaw to Sunderland opening in March 2002. East of Pelaw, the Metro shares the metals with Newcastle–Middlesbrough services as well as heavy freight trains. Beyond Sunderland, the route heads inland along the south bank of the Wear, serving the university and terminating at South Hylton on a route that had closed to passengers in 1964. As well as the stations on the new extension west of Sunderland, the existing BR stations were supplemented by new Metro stations at Fellgate, Stadium of Light and St Peters.

A new bus interchange opened at Park Lane, a month after the other Sunderland stations. Two more Metro stations were to appear on the map; at Northumberland Park in 2005 and Simonside in 2008.

Today's Metro map features two lines; the green line from the airport through Newcastle, Gateshead and Sunderland to South Hylton; and the yellow line from St James through North Tyneside around to South Gosforth where it joins the green line as far as Pelaw, then follows the south bank of the Tyne to South Shields.

More recently, as part of the eleven-year, £350 million 'All Change' modernisation programme, eighty-six Metrocars out of the fleet of ninety were refurbished at Wabtec in Doncaster. They

As with all railways, engineering and maintenance work is essential to keep traffic moving safely and efficiently. This August 2013 scene shows the line just north of Jesmond being re-ballasted and relaid, with various items of mechanical plant in use. Just visible is the junction where the southbound line diverges to the right before it enters the underground section. Continuing straight ahead is the original Blyth & Tyne route, now single track to Manors. (Alex Thorkildsen)

An unusual view of the open end of one of the articulated sections of a Metrocar. Half of No. 4087 is being craned into position to be reunited with her other half, as part of a display at the Gateshead Garden Festival in 1990. (Graham Pearson)

No. 4087 again with all-yellow doors and a broad blue stripe separating the yellow and white bands. This emulated the livery of the local BR 'Pacers', but was not applied across the Metro fleet. The location is West Jesmond. (Graham Pearson)

Metrocar No. 4027 was repainted in North Eastern Railway livery in 2004, to mark the centenary of Britain's first electric suburban railway. Here she is showing off her unique colour scheme, echoing that of the original electric trains, at Pelaw in January 2016. (Scott Lowes)

received a smart monochrome colour scheme with yellow highlights, and Metro staff were issued with new, coordinating grey uniforms at the same time.

Incidentally, whereas the fleet was originally delivered by rail from Metro-Cammell in Birmingham, transport to and from South Yorkshire for refurbishment was undertaken by road, with transfer onto lorries taking place at Hylton Street sidings in North Shields. The four units not taken to Doncaster, Nos 4001, 4002, 4040 and 4083, subsequently had a similar refurbishment carried out at South Gosforth.

Above: Three eras of livery on display in the West Yard of South Gosforth car sheds. From left to right are No. 4001 in the original colour scheme, No. 4025 in the red version of the interim, unrefurbished livery, and No. 4046 in the latest scheme, as photographed 3 May 2014. (Alex Thorkildsen)

Left: Looking through the shed doors into road number 6 at South Gosforth on 5 August 2018 reveals refurbished Metrocar No. 4034. (Scott Lowes)

One of the four Metrocars that were refurbished 'in-house' at South Gosforth is No. 4040. This photograph gives some idea of the extent of the work being done, 5 August 2018. (Scott Lowes)

We have lift-off. A Metrocar is lifted off the rails in its entirety, by the jacks inside South Gosforth car sheds. (Scott Lowes)

Jacking up Metrocar No. 4012 allows maintenance staff to access one of her power bogies, which remains on the rails. The longitudinal traction motor housing can be seen between the wheels. (Scott Lowes)

Several Metrocar axles occupy the foreground of this view inside the workshops at South Gosforth depot. (Scott Lowes)

In January 2007, plans for Metro's future were outlined in the £600 million 'Re-Invigoration of Metro' plan. In expressing the need for investment in Metro, Nexus spelled out the implications for the region of a worst-case scenario where the system was simply allowed to die through failure to invest. Those implications included 15 million more car journeys annually, four times as many buses using the already congested Tyne Bridge, and twice as many buses in Sunderland. It also predicted fewer visitors to the city centres, damaging economic activity.

From 2010, Metro was operated by DB Regio, a subsidiary of Germany's national rail company Deutsche Bahn, but returned to public operation by Nexus in 2017.

One corner of the former Great Northern Railway works at Doncaster is occupied by the workshops of Wabtec, a descendant of Westinghouse Air Brakes. This is where eighty-six Metrocars from the fleet of ninety were refurbished. 1960-built former BR diesel shunter No. 08724 shunts No. 4064 into position prior to work commencing on 3 June 2014. (Alex Thorkildsen)

On 18 August 2014, the peace of Hexthorpe Road in Doncaster is disturbed by the sound of an Allelys Heavy Haulage low-loader, carrying newly refurbished Metrocar No. 4058 as she leaves Wabtec. A 115-mile road journey north will see her safely back on the rails at Hylton Street sidings, North Shields. (Alex Thorkildsen)

Stoddart Street sidings are situated between the East Coast Main Line and the Metro route west of Byker Viaduct, which can be seen curving away to the right. Hunslet battery-electric locomotives BL1 and BL2 have paused here on 4 February 2014, en route from Hylton Street, North Shields to South Gosforth Depot, delivering Metrocar No. 4068, newly refurbished at Doncaster. (Alex Thorkildsen)

A rare view inside the nerve-centre of the Metro. This is South Gosforth Control Centre showing the part of the panel that concerns the nearby depot. (Scott Lowes)

6

Metro – A Cautionary Tale

The 1970s had been a decade of industrial decline for much of Britain, and nowhere more so than in North East England. The beginning of the 1980s promised no brave new world on the economic front, speaking as someone with bitter experience of queueing for unemployment benefit in the North Shields of 1981.

The Metro, our shiny new bright yellow supertram was a ray of sunshine that gripped the imagination of a Tyneside desperate for something to be proud of. I mentioned in the foreword my brother David's best friend, Will, who lived beside us in the street that led to Tynemouth station, and his imagination was certainly gripped. This is his account:

"As a young boy I was given freedoms that kids these days don't experience. Our family lived right next to Tynemouth station, two doors down from my best friend, David. Our days were filled with playing in the wasteland alongside the station which was nicknamed 'The Private'. It was a place to explore, a place to share adventures and excitement, with a *Lord of the Flies* law-of-the-jungle hierarchy.

Before the Metro, Tynemouth station had been out of bounds, as BR staff always chased us off. The idea that the station had a kind of magic about it was elevated in my mind when David,

The exterior of Tynemouth station, on the side where we lived, as did Will's family. The overgrown wasteland was our childhood playground, the former station gardens known to us as "The Private". The prominent tower housed the hydraulic accumulator that powered the luggage hoists at either end of the footbridge. Photo taken *c*. 1981. (Colin Alexander)

swearing me to secrecy, showed me plans for the brand new Metro trams (not trains as my confidant earnestly informed me) that were to replace the noisy, dirty British Rail trains. In my mind, David's Dad invented the Metro, and I'd seen the top-secret documents!

As if a firework exploded in my brain, I became obsessed with everything about the new system. The extensive building work emphasised that big changes were coming and our gang invited ourselves into the temporary signalman's hut where he demonstrated, using cutting edge technology (A grey-painted panel with LEDs and buttons – but hey, it was 1979), where the trams were on the system and if the automatic signalling was working correctly.

He also gave us a brush and let us sweep stuff, which seemed exhilarating at the time. I remember looking through that portacabin window and seeing my first Metro appearing in the distance. It was so stealthy compared to the racket of what had gone before. The yellow of the new supertrams was so bright, the white so clean. The future had arrived.

I remember giving a man who was emptying the ticket machines the 'Spanish Inquisition' on how they worked and how they sorted the coins. He opened the front of the machine revealing tumbling cylinders, flashing lights and giant rolls of tickets looping back and forth like some kind of factory, which was mind-blowing to a young boy.

Traces of the old still lingered though. I remember the sunlight being filtered by the glass canopy, murky from years of billowing diesel fumes, creating a permanent dusk on all but the brightest of days.

All of this meant that I felt very comfortable there; it was my classroom for learning about the world as much as my playground. It was my magic domain. I would ask travellers where they'd been and what that place was like, before asking for their tickets. I must have collected hundreds. If my parents were looking for me, they knew where to find me.

On one occasion I carefully studied an engineer as he worked on the ticket barriers. I started grilling him for information.

Another 1981 photograph shows the automatic ticket vending machines at Tynemouth, with track still in situ in one of the bay platforms beyond. In the distance can be seen the steel footbridge that was intended to replace the original, once demolition of the old station was complete. Thankfully, this was never needed. (Colin Alexander)

Ticket-operated barriers of the original design, as seen at Shiremoor. The photograph shows the turnstile type as well as the wider, gate-opening type for disabled access. (Paul Williams)

What are they for? 'To stop people getting on the platform without a ticket.' How do they work? 'The magnetic strip on the ticket is read by a computer inside, the ticket pops out here and the barrier will turn.' But why do they turn the other way without a ticket? And what happens when they break? And what were they were made of? And how many times did they have to be fixed? And, and, and … it went on for a while as you might imagine.

I had an ambition to collect every possible type of Metro ticket. Soon, I progressed from begging from commuters to grabbing tickets from anywhere possible, even off the ground. Soon though, I had competition. Other kids were after the same yellow prizes.

So I became more inventive (or desperate), searching in bins among cigarette butts and sticky, empty pop cans; or down the back of the ticket machines. One advantage I had over my ticket-collecting rivals was my knowledge of the platform barriers. I found I could retrieve tickets that were stuck in the barriers by crawling inside as it rotated in reverse. I even rescued tickets for passengers who had accidentally lost unused tickets inside the new-fangled contraptions.

I soon gained the upper hand over the competition when I discovered that I could get on the platform without paying and would proudly demonstrate my method. Unfortunately, 'Metro Boy' as my parents had dubbed me, would turn out not to be the superhero suggested by the name.

The sanctity of my 'Metro temple' was desecrated by four scary teenage 'friends' who would appear occasionally. They were ostensibly friendly but even at that tender age I knew they could turn on me any time. They dared me to take a 5p Metro journey on my own to Monkseaton, which required a rescue from my ever-patient Dad.

In my seven-year-old mind I thought I could vanquish my teenage tormentors and make them go away forever, but that is not how it played out. They called me out on my boast that I could get through the barrier and onto the platform, so thinking that victory was in sight I set about demonstrating my technique.

Catastrophically, at the moment I should have got my entire body between the stainless bars of the unit I somehow managed to get only my head into the cavity, with my body on the other side of the turnstile. I was sure that my 'friends' had somehow caused this calamity.

I could sense a flurry of activity behind me but just as quickly they were gone. My senses were slipping from my grasp, and I was thrashing to hold onto my life. Panic took hold, I was struggling, gasping and choking all at once. The more I tried to free myself the tighter the bar gripped my neck. I heard a kind voice trying to calm me. It seemed stupid, what did she know? I was trying to tell her how the barrier worked, but I couldn't speak, I couldn't breathe. But my dad was coming I knew that, I'd heard someone say it. She said lift my legs. Was she mad?! I kicked and I struggled some more.

METRO BOY IN TERROR TRAP

He passes out in barrier drama

FIRE BRIGADE CALLED TO WILLIAM THE WORRY

'Just William' in Metro jam

METRO-MAD William Walker was back home yesterday after his fascination with Tyneside's new train system almost cost him his life.

The seven-year-old was collecting used Metro tickets at Tynemouth Station—just yards from his home in Shipley Road—when disaster struck.

Blond-haired William tripped and managed to get his head stuck fast in a ticket turnstile.

He turned blue in the face as breathing became difficult and eventually passed out before being freed by the fire brigade and taken to Preston Hospital, North Shields, where he was detained overnight.

When only six, William—nicknamed "Just William" because of his scrapes—managed to buy himself Metro tickets and ride to the Haymarket and back.

And recently his father found him getting off at Tynemouth after a trip to Monkseaton.

His father said: "He has been absolutely Metro-mad since it first opened. He is fascinated by everything about it.

Some of the local newspaper cuttings from the time of 'Metro Boy' Will Walker's brush with death at Tynemouth station. This was May 1981. (Will Walker)

Then he was here, my Dad. He could fix this, he could do anything, it was going to be okay. But even with my senses confused I knew his tools were having no impact on the metal frame, the discordant screech of a hacksaw blade sliding powerlessly against steel, its vibrations passing into my body through my strangled neck. My Dad's almighty but futile effort to rip the machine apart mingling with his desperation, his agony, his love, his fear of the death of his son. Then for me there was just fading, from that desperate dusk, to black, then to nothing.

When I opened my eyes, I could see the ornate framework of the canopy, framed by silhouettes of heads and breathing apparatus arched over me. As life flooded back into me, I understood I was alive. My dad held me in his arms. I wanted him to never let go. The fire brigade had arrived while I was unconscious and tore the machine apart, but I lay there without a pulse and without life. At that moment a Metro had swept into the gloom and delivered a saviour; a doctor stepped from the gleaming tram and instantly breathed life into me with his own. The miracle of the clean, efficient and speedy Metro system had saved me, without it, that doctor would have not arrived in time.

I am pleased to say that after years of trying to find Audrey McCebe, the kindly spoken lady described in a local paper as my rescue heroine, we were recently reunited. I was able to thank her in person for calming me down and finding my dad. By adding those minutes to the time I had left she saved my life. But I would like to say it in print too, so, Audrey, thank you, the world is a better place with lovely caring people like you in it.

I'd also like to thank the anonymous NHS doctor who knew exactly what to do, and our brave Fire and Rescue service whose work is often unrecognised and who turn out in the most desperate of circumstances.

I remember only a few weeks later, tragically, another boy* died in an almost identical incident. The platform barriers were removed from all but the staffed stations after that. Unsurprisingly, Tynemouth Metro station was no longer my Magic Kingdom. My near-death experience made me realise that this was not a safe place to be for so many reasons, but I still hold wonderful childhood memories from that time."

Will's account graphically brings to life the magic and newness of the Metro when it opened, but also illustrates some of the dangers to which children can be exposed.

Happily, following their reunion, Will and Audrey were interviewed in November 2019 on BBC Radio Newcastle about the events of that day thirty-eight years ago.

---

*Ten-year-old Roger Walker from Surrey, staying with relatives in Newcastle, died at Benton station in August 1982, in very similar circumstances to Will's accident.

7

Metro Journey

A journey on the 'yellow' line begins in the city centre at St James, where the entrance to the underground station is situated below the Gallowgate end of Newcastle United's ground. The football club was established here in 1892 but today's towering stadium is unrecognisable compared to the crumbling edifice that occupied the site for many decades. The Metro station concourse features a gallery of photos of Magpies legends as well as a miniature pitch with famous footballing footprints and goalkeepers' handprints in relief.

We descend the escalator into the surprisingly cavernous station where the football theme continues with black and white panelling and giant photographs of the 'Toon Army' faithful. This underground terminus has short lengths of dead-end tunnel to the west, designed for possible future extension. Trains arriving at St James are subject to automatic braking to ensure there is no repeat of the tragic 1975 Moorgate disaster in London, in which a tube train travelling at more than 30 mph ran into a similar 'blind' over-run tunnel, killing forty-three people including the driver. Its cause remains a mystery.

As we commence our journey around the Metro network and descend the escalator to one of the platforms at St James, we can appreciate the cavernous nature of the station. (Colin Alexander)

Sporting the blue version of the pre-refurbishment livery, Metrocars No. 4024 and No. 4047 await departure from St James with a service for South Shields on 13 June 2014. (Alex Thorkildsen)

A photograph taken in December 2014 showing the smart interior of refurbished prototype Metrocar No. 4001 in St James' bright, modern-looking station. (Alex Thorkildsen)

The original plan for St James station incorporated a third platform, of which vestiges can be seen, although it was never operational.

Back to our coastbound journey. If we are lucky, we can claim the front seats beside the driving cab, which only occupies half of the train's width. Tunnelling beneath Newcastle city centre, our first stop is at Monument, named after the column topped by the statue of Earl Grey, whose Great Reform Act of 1832 changed British politics forever.

Monument is by far the busiest station on the Metro, followed by Haymarket and Central station. The ticket concourse was constructed around the foundations of the famous landmark, and following the curved wall formed by this leads to an exit directly into Eldon Square shopping centre, which at the time of its opening in 1976 was the largest in the UK. There are also exits to Blackett Street and the beautiful Grey Street, voted Britain's best street by BBC Radio 4's 'Today' listeners. A recent addition is a walkway from the concourse into the basement of Fenwick's, the legendary Newcastle department store, famous for its Christmas window display.

Around the street-level exits from Monument station are one of Metro's more subtle artworks. This is Richard Cole's 'Circuit', an abstract design based on microelectronic symbols, sandblasted on pavements and walls. Further along Blackett Street and away from the station

First of the production series, Metrocar No. 4003 leads No. 4026 as they climb the gradient out of the tunnel at Manors on their way from St James via Tynemouth and Benton to South Shields on 4 May 2014. The East Coast Main Line to Edinburgh is alongside, with the solitary remaining island platform of Manors' former BR station in the background. (Alex Thorkildsen)

Soon after exiting the tunnel from Manors our train soars over the Ouseburn on the Byker viaduct, the eastern end of which is seen in this 1980s view. Part of the Byker Wall housing development is in the right background. (D. R. Dunn collection)

entrances is David Hamilton's 'Parsons' Polygon', a terracotta tribute to Charles Parsons of Turbinia fame, which is actually the ventilation shaft for the underground station, in disguise.

Next stop is Manors, which was one of the Metro's less used stations in its early days, but where patronage has increased as it serves the newest part of Northumbria University, whose students may admire the lively station concourse murals by Basil Beattie. Above ground nearby, are the sad remains of the former NER Manors station, which once boasted nine platforms.

The Metro line climbs to the surface to emerge alongside the East Coast Main Line at the point where the North Eastern Railway's Quayside branch formerly plunged into a steeply graded and tightly curved tunnel down to the Tyne. Part of that company's pioneering electrification scheme, the NER had two electric locomotives especially built for this route in 1903, and one of them survives in the National Railway Museum.

We may be lucky enough to 'race' a main-line train on the adjacent Ouseburn Viaduct while our Metrocar soars gracefully over the valley on the slender, curving Byker Viaduct.

We arrive at Byker station beside Ralph Erskine's iconic and innovative 'Byker Wall' housing development of the 1970s. This was one of Tyneside's more successful slum-clearance projects, and avoided the mistakes made by 1960s tower-block developers. Leaving Byker, we curve through a tunnel and another cutting to arrive at Chillingham Road, beside the main-line sidings at Heaton Junction, where there is another opportunity to see an Anglo-Scottish express speeding past.

Looking west in the direction of the viaduct and daylight, we see Metrocar No. 4085 in the red version of the interim livery along with No. 4055 at Byker station with a St James to South Shields service, on 26 October 2013. (Alex Thorkildsen)

Leaving Byker, we pass through a tunnel then a deep cutting in which Metrocar No. 4087 is seen leaving Chillingham Road towards St James in November 1983. Several BR freight wagons are visible in the background, in the sidings at Heaton Junction. (Paul Williams)

The telephoto lens accentuating the changes in gradient, Metrocar No. 4056 slows for *Suggestus 2* (Latin for platform 2!) at Wallsend in July 2013 as it heads a St James service. (Colin Alexander)

With station and train showing the original colour scheme to good effect, Metrocar No. 4052 arrives at Hadrian Road, on its way from St James to Heworth in June 1984. (Paul Williams)

Constructed in 1837–1839 from laminated timber beams for the Newcastle & North Shields Railway, the spans of John Green's viaduct over Willington Dene were rebuilt in iron in 1869, by the Weardale Iron & Coal Co. Robert Stephenson was born in nearby Willington Quay in 1803. (Colin Alexander)

Autumn is leaf-fall season, causing rail adhesion problems everywhere. Just like Network Rail, Nexus operates a rail-head treatment train (RHTT), seen here passing Howdon on 14 October 2015 on its way from Chillingham Road to South Gosforth. It is powered by Metrocar No. 4070 and battery-electric locomotive BL2. The cloud of spray and the debris being dislodged can be seen below the train. (Alex Thorkildsen)

Our route so far has been entirely new and purpose-built, opening in late 1982. From Chillingham Road we will follow the course of the Newcastle & North Shields Railway, which opened in 1839, meaning that the Metro can stake a claim to be the oldest commuter railway in the world.

Walkergate and Wallsend stations follow, both built as new Metro halts on the sites of existing, dilapidated BR stations that were mostly of timber construction. Wallsend is, of course, named for its location at the eastern end of Hadrian's Wall, and Segedunum Roman fort is nearby, with its reconstructions of a section of full-height wall and a Roman bath house overlooking the former Swan Hunter slipways, where so many famous ships were launched. The modern observation platform, which gives an aerial view of the recently excavated fort, is a prominent landmark.

Because of the Roman connection, Wallsend's Metro station boasts the only Latin signage on any British railway station; the work of artist Michael Pinsky, with translations such as *Suggestus 1* for Platform 1, and *Noli Fumare* warning passengers not to smoke.

Continuing in a straight-line eastward, we are able to view a stretch of the Tyne where former shipyards now build the platforms for offshore wind farms.

Our next call is Hadrian Road before we cross Willington Dene on John Green's viaduct, rebuilt in 1869 in iron, replacing the original 1839 laminated timbers. It is over 300 metres long and 25 metres above Wallsend Burn, and is of similar design to his Ouseburn Viaduct, seen earlier.

Our next stop, Howdon, differs from the other stations so far, in that its platforms are staggered. This is so that trains are always stationary before they proceed over the automatic level crossing on Howdon Lane. My Great Uncle Harry was a signalman here in LNER and early BR days, and he used to turn the wheel that operated the old mechanical level crossing gates from the signal-box. Today there are no gates or barriers, only flashing lights and audible warnings.

Leaving Howdon, we soon pass the site where a temporary Metro depot is being constructed, about which there is more in chapter 8.

Before we reach Percy Main, we cross the A19's northern approach to the Tyne Tunnel, an earlier attempt to ease Tyneside's traffic congestion. Before it opened in 1967, the only vehicular crossing downstream of the Tyne Bridge was the car ferry between North and South Shields. To our right we may observe another bridge over the A19, which once carried the track-bed of the NER's Riverside branch, which converged with the main North Tyne loop at Percy Main.

Another overbridge carries us across the North Tyneside Steam Railway, whose northern terminus is the former Metro Test Centre. Just north of the Metro station we can see the stone-built Percy Arms, now a restaurant, whose upper rear windows once looked out on the Blyth & Tyne Railway station of 1844.

Percy Main was also the place where the 'Norseman' boat-train from London King's Cross branched off for the Tyne Commission Quay. Perusal of an old Ordnance Survey map of this stretch of the river, with the Northumberland Dock and Albert Edward Dock, now known as Royal Quays, reveals a vast network of railway sidings and staithes, where coal was shipped, and timber pit-props were unloaded. My Dad used to take me there to watch NCB steam engines shunting, and to see the glamorous ships like the *Braemar* and *Leda*, bound for Scandinavia. All of this, along with the former Percy Main engine shed, is long-gone, although it is still possible to board a ferry across the North Sea.

Meadow Well, previously known as Smith's Park, is our next stop, then on the right we pass the sidings at Hylton Street, which were used to transfer Metro vehicles to and from road transport during the refurbishment programme.

The once foreboding and enclosed station at North Shields is considerably brighter nowadays, following a recent rebuild. Should passengers wish to do so, a walk down the hill to the river will bring them to the pedestrian ferry landing for the crossing to South Shields, or a stroll along the revitalised Fish Quay to view the four lighthouses, the earliest of which dates back to 1727.

Eighteen months earlier than the previous photograph, on 4 February 2014, No. 4070 was at Hylton Street sidings, North Shields, on her way to Wabtec at Doncaster for refurbishment. In the background, Hunslet battery-electric locomotives BL1 and BL2 prepare to take No. 4068, just arrived from Doncaster, back to South Gosforth to rejoin her sisters. (Alex Thorkildsen)

North Shields' platform 3 was used when 'blue line' trains terminated here from St James. That service ended before 2002 in order to free up Metrocars for the South Hylton route, so this visit of car No. 4081 in 2009 was a rarity. (Richard Vogel)

North Shields station was an eyesore in BR days, having lost its original overall arched roof, and with a collection of 1960s 'prefabs' serving as a station building. Its first Metro incarnation was little better, incorporating much of the existing fabric. Happily, it was rebuilt in 2012, and the striking new structure is seen here in 2013 with Metrocars Nos 4084 and 4038 advertising the now defunct East Coast rail franchise. (Richard Vogel)

A typical, vibrant weekend scene under Tynemouth station's 200-metre-long Victorian iron and glass canopy, with the market in full swing, July 2014. Compare this to the condition of the station buildings as depicted in the previous chapter. (Colin Alexander)

Remaining on the Metro, the route takes us through a cutting and a series of 'cut-and-cover' tunnels, the first of which is 720 metres long. This was the 1847 Tynemouth extension, opened by the Newcastle and Berwick Railway, which had absorbed the Newcastle & North Shields Railway in 1844.

Once out of the cutting we cross the bridge over Tanners Bank, which leads down to the Fish Quay, and pass the site of the Blyth and Tyne Railway's 1860 terminus station, which was just east of the Tynemouth Lodge pub.

Just before our Metro curves northwards beneath Tynemouth Road, directly ahead of us is the site of the Newcastle and Berwick Railway's original 1847 Tynemouth terminus, whose main building survives on Oxford Street. It was designed by Benjamin Green and is architecturally similar to his intermediate stations on the Newcastle to Berwick main line. Although it closed to passengers in 1882, its sidings remained in use until the late 1970s as a coal yard. It also used to have an inclined connection to the railway that ran along the North Pier at the mouth of the Tyne.

Soon, we arrive in Tynemouth's splendid North Eastern Railway station of 1882. Designed to cope with holiday traffic as well as commuters, it once boasted four tracks between its through platforms as well as several bay platforms, all under an extensive glass canopy. Tynemouth was well-known as a 'watering place' with its sandy beaches and lofty cliffs, topped by the dramatic, romantic ruins of its priory and castle, once painted by JMW Turner.

Tynemouth's NER station replaced the termini of the Blyth & Tyne and the Newcastle & Berwick, both of which had by then been absorbed by the NER. By that time there was a second B&TR Tynemouth terminus, which had opened in 1865 across the road from Oxford Street, approximately where the Territorial Army has its premises. The track-bed of the connection to the old B&TR route can be seen curving south-westward under the bridge beneath Mariners Lane.

When the neglected shell of Tynemouth station passed from BR to Metro ownership, it was scheduled to be demolished and replaced by a simple, modern Metro halt, while the remainder of the site was to be redeveloped. Thankfully, this caused a public outcry, and a group named Friends of Tynemouth Station was formed, supported by Tynemouth Village Association. With the backing of North Tyneside Council and the Fine Arts Commission, the public campaign led by the redoubtable Ylana First MBE, saved the great Victorian edifice with its magnificent glazed roof and unique footbridge. Incidentally, in the 1970s I received a £5 reward from British Rail for reporting a fire I had noticed taking hold in the timbers of the bridge.

The bridge is in three sections and has four staircases. Between the two covered pedestrian walkways that gently arch over the track, there is a flat, wide, enclosed bridge that was once used by barrows for the conveyance of parcels and holidaymakers' luggage. It employed hydraulic hoists at each end, powered by an accumulator housed in the station's prominent tower. The light, airy space in the centre of the footbridge hosts ever-changing art installations.

Following its multi-million-pound renovation, the Grade II* listed building, designed by NER architect William Bell, hosts a vibrant market every weekend and its spacious buildings contain a restaurant, a great little pub and other businesses. As I grew up next to Tynemouth station, and passed through it every day on my way to and from school, it thrills me that 'people power' saved her from destruction. In her North Eastern Railway heyday, she won several best-kept station prizes and she is now, in my opinion, the jewel in the crown of our Metro.

We now head north along the NER 1882 route, which replaced the Blyth & Tyne Railway's Tynemouth branch. This ran parallel, about a mile inland. We can enjoy views of North Sea shipping, Tynemouth Park, the Art Deco Park Hotel, the aquarium and St George's Church as we approach Cullercoats. The station here is a contemporary of her larger sister at Tynemouth and is home to a large photographic artwork by Cathy de Monchaux, depicting a station in Paris. It is a short walk from here to the charming Cullercoats Bay with its caves and lifeboat station.

It takes hardly any time at all for our Metro to cover the distance from Cullercoats to Whitley Bay, whose station was rebuilt in 1910 to cope with increasing holiday traffic, and retains many original features including an impressive clock tower. Much of that traffic

The spacious, light and airy nature of Tynemouth station can be appreciated as test track stalwart No. 4002, wearing a special 'Metro Days Out' livery arrives with a St James service in 2013. The late twentieth century business units on the opposite platform look somewhat incongruous. (Colin Alexander)

The unique and original double footbridge at Tynemouth, soon after refurbishment of the station was completed, in 2013. (Colin Alexander)

Architecturally similar to its contemporary, larger sister, Tynemouth, Cullercoats station also retains much of its original character, including the original wooden footbridge. Metrocars Nos 4035 and 4063 are on their way from South Shields to St James on 23 December 2019. (Colin Alexander)

originated in Glasgow during 'Fairs Fortnight' when flocks of Clydesiders crammed into special trains bound for the North Sea coast. Locomotive-hauled excursions from Scotland continued until the late 1970s. Modern mosaics of seaside scenes by Ian Patience adorn the former booking hall.

Whitley Bay was once a bustling seaside resort with its Spanish City amusement park, featured in the Dire Straits song *Tunnel of Love*. Although the dodgems and rollercoaster are long-gone, the recently beautifully restored white dome is a well-loved landmark, and is a great place to go for food, drink and sea views towards St Mary's Island with its iconic white lighthouse and seal colony.

Monkseaton's spacious station dates from 1915 and was the junction for the Blyth & Tyne Railway's Avenue branch, which diverged here towards Blyth. The southbound platform retains its original arched overall roof and buildings, which include a delightful micro-pub. A pleasant time can be spent over a pint, admiring Mike Davies' stained-glass beach and shipyard scenes in the end screens of the glass canopy.

Continuing inland, the simplicity of West Monkseaton's Art Deco architecture gives away its 1930s origins, being built by the LNER to serve Whitley Bay's spreading suburbs.

As we speed across the open fields after West Monkseaton; to the north is the prominent landmark of St Alban's Church, Earsdon. Its graveyard contains the poignant memorial to the

Whitley Bay's iconic clock tower has, since 1910, been a beacon for homeward-bound seaside daytrippers and Glaswegian holidaymakers. The sea front is half a kilometre away down Station Road and Esplanade. (Colin Alexander)

The ironwork of the North Eastern Railway's 1910 Whitley Bay station is not as ornate as that at Tynemouth, but its survival is equally pleasing. Metrocars Nos 4086 and 4036 are on their way from St James to South Shields on St Valentine's Day 2014. (Alex Thorkildsen)

The rail-head treatment train does not always employ the Hunslet battery-electric locomotives. Approaching Whitley Bay on 6 November 2016 are prototype Metrocar No. 4001, still in PTE colours, and refurbished No. 4060 as they travel the circular route from South Gosforth and back via the Manors curve and the old Jesmond station. (Alex Thorkildsen)

One of Mike Davies' stained-glass installations can be seen on the end screen of Monkseaton's 1915-built arched canopy. This one depicts a shipyard (Colin Alexander)

Hartley pit disaster of 1862, in which 204 men and boys perished when the beam of the engine broke and blocked the only shaft. Beyond the church, on a clear day, can be seen the distant Cheviots on the Scottish border. Where else can you view both sea and mountains in the space of ten minutes, from an 'underground' train? Any passenger glancing across the fields in the opposite direction here would be forgiven for thinking a giant spaceship, with Lego bricks scattered on the roof, had landed. This is in fact Monkseaton High School, built in 2009.

The next stop, Shiremoor, opened in 1980, replacing the less conveniently located former BR station at Backworth, further west. Northumberland Park is a more recent addition opened in 2005, just beyond site of Backworth station, serving an extensive area of new housing development. Alongside the station, the freight-only former Blyth & Tyne Railway route to Blyth and Lynemouth trails in from the north.

We are now travelling along the route of the B&TR 1864 Newcastle branch, parallel to the freight line as we continue west to Palmersville station, added to the network in 1986. A mile to the north, in Killingworth, is George Stephenson's Dial Cottage, where he and his son Robert began their railway revolution. After Palmersville, the Metro route climbs over the freight line as the latter descends the curve to join the East Coast Main Line, which we cross before arriving at Benton station, built by the Blyth & Tyne in 1871.

On 2 March 2014, services between Shiremoor and St James were suspended for engineering work. Metrocar No. 4064, carrying the name *Michael Campbell,* and unnamed No. 4051 have just used the crossover east of Shiremoor station, where passengers will be picked up before heading for South Shields. (Alex Thorkildsen)

Northumberland Park station is one of the later additions to the Metro network. A pair of Metrocars led by refurbished No. 4067 calls here on 11 November 2017 with a South Shields service. The third, unelectrified track on the left is the freight-only line to North Blyth and Bedlington. It is hoped that one day passenger services will return to this route. (Scott Lowes)

Before Northumberland Park was thought of, Palmersville station was added between Shiremoor and Benton to serve residential developments that appeared after the line opened in 1980. It was almost new when Metrocar No. 4031 and a sister unit called there on their way to Pelaw in May 1986. (Paul Williams)

The small shelter on the left and station building on the right are original structures from the Blyth & Tyne Railway's Benton station built in 1871. Metrocar No. 4045 is in a colour scheme to commemorate the seventy-fifth anniversary of Newcastle Airport, and together with NER-liveried No. 4027 it makes a colourful combination as they run empty from Monkseaton to South Gosforth depot on 13 June 2014. (Alex Thorkildsen)

It is possible to discern the track-beds of former curves that once connected the North Tyne loop with the main line from west to north and west to south, just east of Benton station. The south-west curve survived until the late 1980s for BR freight traffic.

Shortly after leaving Benton, we slow for the bus interchange at Four Lane Ends. Another short hop brings us to Longbenton, the last station to be built by the LNER, in 1947, a year before nationalisation. It was built specifically to serve the nearby 'Ministry', otherwise known as the Department for Work and Pensions. The post-war style of austere 1940s architecture is enlivened by 'Journey's Echo', an artwork by Elinor Eastwood in collaboration with local sixth-form students; as well as the colourfully tiled footbridge artwork of Simon Jones and Rob Belilios.

Having travelled west for some time, our train now negotiates a sharp curve left and makes a beeline for the city centre, still following the former Blyth & Tyne Railway. As we take the curve, we can see South Gosforth car sheds on our right. Built in 1923 to house the North Eastern Railway's electric trains, replacing the fire-damaged Heaton car sheds, it later maintained Tyneside's DMU fleet before being inherited by the Tyne & Wear Metro.

As we take the curve after Longbenton on the right we can catch a glimpse of South Gosforth depot. Here, on 12 October 2013, battery-electric BL2 and BL1 prepare to take No. 4063 to Hylton Street for transfer to a low-loader for the road journey to Doncaster for refurbishment. (Alex Thorkildsen)

The standard-pattern North Eastern Railway footbridge is all that remains of South Gosforth's old station. One corner of the Control Centre is visible top left in this 2015 view of unrefurbished No. 4040 arriving from the coast. Identical footbridges removed from Percy Main and Howdon in the early 1980s are now at the National Railway Museum in York, and Goathland on the North Yorkshire Moors Railway, respectively. (Colin Alexander)

The Airport branch now trails in from the right as we arrive at South Gosforth station. This retains its North Eastern Railway footbridge, which contrasts with the modern 1970s architecture of the Metro Control Centre. Here, passengers from the coast can change onto airport trains, and vice versa.

It is little more than 2 miles from here to the city centre, but there are four stops to make before we reach the 'hub' of the network beneath Grey's Monument. First is Ilford Road, an archetypal, minimalist Metro halt where previously British Rail trains passed non-stop. This is a convenient station for a stroll down into Jesmond Dene, the leafy urban park gifted to the people of Newcastle by the great industrialist Lord Armstrong.

Next is West Jesmond, which retains some of its original buildings. These are of red brick and date from 1900. Soon, we enter the north–south underground section at Jesmond. As our train veers right and dives into the subterranean station, a single track continues straight ahead through the original 1864 Blyth & Tyne Railway Jesmond station, which survives as a charming pub, complete with a former Great Northern Railway coach and a replica signal-box on the platform, serving as a restaurant.

Positively glowing in the spring sunshine, Nos 4003 and 4026 approach West Jesmond station en route from St James to South Shields on 11 March 2014. (Alex Thorkildsen)

About to enter the underground section at Jesmond are South Tyneside-bound Metrocars Nos 4012 and 4077 on 23 October 2013. The cant of the track around the curve is clearly visible. (Alex Thorkildsen)

unrefurbished train, refurbished station. This is the new-look Haymarket with Nos 4026 and 4045 forming a train from Pelaw to Regent Centre on 9 February 2015. (Alex Thorkildsen)

More than thirty years after its opening, the clean, bright condition of Monument station is testament to the quality of design and materials at the time of building. Metrocars Nos 4037 and 4055 are on their way from South Shields to St James on 16 May 2014. (Alex Thorkildsen)

This single line is retained as a connection to the east–west route at Manors which it reaches via a short, sharply curved tunnel, providing empty trains with a shortcut between the St James end of the line and South Gosforth depot. Meanwhile, having called at the 'new' Jesmond station of 1980, with its Simon Butler murals at platform level and Raf Fulcher's sculpture garden above ground, we descend deeper under the city, where we reach the newly refurbished Haymarket station. This rebuilding was part of the 'All Change' modernisation programme.

Haymarket was the original city terminus at the time of the 1980 opening, and serves the northern end of the shopping district, a large bus station and the city's two universities. The station's new look features Lothar Goetz's vibrant, abstract colour scheme. Passengers who exit here cannot fail to notice one of Newcastle's most iconic landmarks, the Civic Centre, designed by George Kenyon and opened in 1968.

Monument is our next stop, where our southbound train calls at a platform 7 metres below the east–west route negotiated less than an hour earlier, after we left St James. Visitors alighting here can admire the 1830s architecture of Grey Street and Grainger Street, which descend from the Monument towards the Tyne and the Central station, respectively. The great Tyneside architect John Dobson was responsible for much of this splendour, as he was for the Central station, which is our next stop.

Daniel Wright said of the new corporate monochrome scheme with yellow accents, "it is quite brilliant, putting Calvert's iconic typeface and Metro's traditional yellow centre-stage, but presented in a clean and crisp manner with a visual integrity that meets modern expectations". This is the refurbished Central station in 2017. (Colin Alexander)

Part of the Thomas Bewick-inspired mural by Hilary Paynter at concourse level inside Central station. This section depicts a Metro 'beacon' in front of the Byker Wall, St James Park, the mouth of the Tyne, Tynemouth Priory, the Tyne bridges, Swan Hunter's shipyard and Hadrian's Wall. (Colin Alexander)

Like Haymarket, the Metro station here has recently benefited from rebuilding. Above the escalators, as we emerge into the main-line Central station, the panelling is adorned by Hilary Paynter's monochrome Tyneside scenes, inspired by the engravings of the great Thomas Bewick; as well as Steve McNulty's colourful 'Wakes Week' mural. This leads us into Dobson's superb station, dating from the 1840s and one of only five Grade I listed railway stations outside of London.

Its east end used to be the departure point for trains over what is now the Metro network. Those former suburban platforms are now a car park. Beside the Metro exit into the main line station is the Centurion bar, which is well worth a visit. It was formerly the First Class Refreshment Room in NER days, and has been restored to its Victorian splendour.

When Central station was built, it was truly central to the commercial centre of the town (Newcastle was not granted city status until 1882), but by the 1980s the city had expanded northwards and today's underground Metro stations serve its commuters and shoppers much more effectively. Much of that historic centre survives, thankfully, and the mediaeval town walls, quayside, cathedral and castle can be explored from here.

Leaving Central, we burrow under Forth Street, a hive of industry in the 1820s when *Locomotion No. 1* and *Rocket* were built in the world's first locomotive works, Robert Stephenson & Company, which has recently been restored.

Suddenly, we burst into daylight to cross the River Tyne on the middle one of three railway bridges. Situated between Stephenson's double-decked High Level Bridge of 1849 and Charles Harrison's King Edward VII Bridge of 1906, the Metro's Queen Elizabeth II Bridge was opened in 1981. It is illuminated by Nayan Kulkarni's 'Nocturne' installation. The artist designed it so that different coloured messages pass backwards and forwards across the river at a speed and intensity determined by the Tyne's tidal flow. It complements the design of the bridge and pays tribute to Sunderland-born Joseph Swan, the inventor of the electric light bulb. It was thanks to him that in 1879, Mosley Street in Newcastle became the world's first electrically lit street.

The scale of the Queen Elizabeth II Bridge can be appreciated in this 2016 view looking west from Gateshead. Beyond it is the King Edward VII Bridge, built in 1906 to obviate the need for Anglo-Scottish trains to reverse at Newcastle. The Redheugh Bridge, which opened to road traffic in the early 1980s, is just upstream of the railway bridge. (Colin Alexander)

Gateshead station is not quite as cavernous as St James, but it is more open than most underground stations, being built inside an old quarry. The brightly lit, colourful, modern, tiled stations were a breath of fresh air for Tyneside's commuters when they opened in the early 1980s, compared to the shabby, vandalised facilities they replaced. (Colin Alexander)

On the left, beyond the High Level Bridge, we can also see the Tyne Bridge of 1928, Armstrong's Swing Bridge of 1876 and the Millennium Bridge of 2000. The Baltic Centre for Contemporary Art and the Sage music venue are prominent landmarks on Gateshead Quayside. On a sunny day when the Tyne is still and mirror-like, this is one of the most stunning, dramatic scenes to be beheld from a train carriage.

No sooner have we crossed the river than we plunge underground once more, beneath the site of the North Eastern Railway's Greenesfield Works and Gateshead engine sheds, now consigned to history.

The former BR Gateshead East and West stations, at the south end of the High Level Bridge, were replaced by the more conveniently-located Gateshead interchange.

This is the largest of the purpose-built Metro/bus interchanges and its deep-level platforms are brightened up by Keith Grant's 'Night and Day' mosaics at either end. Another of his mosaics can be seen in the concourse above. Outside, between the bus stands is Danny Lane's massive sculpture in steel and glass.

The underground route continues east and reaches the surface at Gateshead Stadium (originally to have been called Old Fold) station, alongside the Network Rail route to Sunderland. In his heyday, local lad Steve Cram would have been able to cover the 800 m from the station to the famous athletics stadium in one-minute and forty-two seconds. The stadium is also synonymous with the great distance runner, Brendan Foster, who founded the annual Great North Run which generates so many extra Metro passengers, be they spectators or exhausted half-marathon runners on their weary but triumphant way home from South Shields.

Beyond the stadium and across the Tyne we can see the distinctive outline of the Byker Wall, and further east some of the now-dormant shipyard cranes that have been a landmark for decades.

Back in daylight, having emerged above ground at Gateshead Stadium, we meet the Test Track twins again. Prototypes Nos 4001 and 4002 approach Felling on their way from the airport to South Hylton on 9 February 2015. Above the centre of the train, St James Park dominates the city skyline. (Alex Thorkildsen)

In my childhood we seemed to have heavy snowfalls every winter. Nowadays this is a rare occurrence, especially in October. Felling station is the location as Nos 4031 and 4062 form an Airport to South Hylton service on 23 October 2013. (Alex Thorkildsen)

Visible from the platform at Felling is one of the oldest surviving station buildings in the world. The Brandling Junction Railway opened its Felling station in 1839 and it is seen here on 30 December 2019. Liverpool Road station in Manchester is the world's oldest, dating from 1830. (Colin Alexander)

As we leave the next stop, Felling, eagle-eyed passengers will notice a tiny, Gothic stone building on the north side of the railway. This was Felling's first station on the Brandling Junction Railway, which had opened in 1839 from Gateshead to Brockley Whins. On its gable is a coat of arms, prophetically accompanied by the initials 'BR', for Brandling Railway, as opposed to British Railways.

After Felling comes Heworth interchange, which opened to BR trains in 1979 and Metro in 1981. It was the southern terminus of Metro services until the South Shields line was opened, and allows interchange between Metro, buses and 'heavy rail' services to Sunderland and Teesside. The building features two major artworks: Mike Clay's 'South Tyne Eye Plan' depicts local scenes in a format inspired by old stagecoach route maps; and outside, Jenny Cowern's 'Things Made' is a mural inspired by historic local industries.

The Metro route here was part of the original main line from London to Edinburgh, until the shorter route through Durham and the Team Valley was opened in 1872. Pelaw station, added to the Metro network in 1985, was once a three-way junction with the former Leamside line diverging to our right towards Washington. This line closed to passengers in 1963 and altogether in 1991, though its track-bed has been considered as a possible future Metro route.

We can see the Sunderland line heading straight on from Pelaw but our train curves left and runs roughly parallel with the meandering River Tyne. From here to just beyond Jarrow,

Just east of Heworth interchange, Metrocars Nos 4005 and 4001 are on their way from South Hylton to the airport on 2 May 2014. The unelectrified running lines to the left form Network Rail's Newcastle to Sunderland and Teesside route. (Alex Thorkildsen)

Pelaw station opened in 1985 and features a striking curved, sloping canopy. Metrocar No. 4004 in green livery has stopped at the island platform there on 31 January 2016, en route for Wearside. (Scott Lowes)

we travel on single track, with passing loops at the stations. Clearly visible across the Tyne is the 200-foot hammerhead crane of the former Walker Naval Yard, dating from 1930, and the biggest in England. It was used in the building of the battleship *King George V* and aircraft carriers *Ark Royal* and *Illustrious*. This part of Walker Riverside, along with much of the Tyne and the Port of Blyth is now a hub for the UK's renewable energy technology sector.

We travel along the 1872 NER route through Hebburn station to Jarrow, where Vince Rae's sculpture commemorates the famous Jarrow March of 1936. Rather poignantly, given the context of that historical event, it is made from steel recycled from a scrapped ship. Both Hebburn and Jarrow stations stand on the sites of their BR predecessors.

Just after leaving Jarrow we get a good view of the southern entrance to the Tyne Tunnels, the second of which opened in 2011, doubling its capacity. As well as the famous march, Jarrow is known for its ruined monastery, home to the Venerable Bede. The tower of the adjacent St Paul's Church can be seen below the giant pylons that carry high voltage high over the Tyne and its shipping. A kilometre away from the monastery is our next station, named Bede after the ancient scholar. It welcomed its first passengers when the South Shields Metro line opened in 1984. Simonside station is newer still, following in 2008. The train then passes through the curved Tyne Dock Tunnel before arriving at Tyne Dock station. This replaced its BR namesake, a location once synonymous with giant coal-handling facilities for export, a situation which is now reversed.

From here to the bus interchange at Chichester (whose first syllable rhymes with 'tie'), the Metro route follows not the NER 1872 South Shields branch, but an even earlier route. We are now running on a track-bed which, from 1834, carried trains of the Stanhope & Tyne Railway, engineered by George Stephenson. He would be impressed by the modern concrete viaduct that carries us up to the new station at South Shields. As we approach, we can see the impressive

The foot crossing at South Drive, between Hebburn and Pelaw, is the setting for this photograph of Nos 4084 and 4049 working a South Shields to St James service on 23 October 2013. The extra line on the left is Network Rail's freight-only Jarrow branch. (Alex Thorkildsen)

The steel sculpture of Vince Rae's *Jarrow March* is visible on the left, as Nos 4026 and 4003 call at Jarrow with a South Shields to St James train on 14 June 2014. (Alex Thorkildsen)

The colourful pairing of Nos 4045 and 4027 again, this time at Simonside with a St James to South Shields service on 26 July 2014. (Alex Thorkildsen)

A train for St James, via Gateshead, Benton and Tynemouth, awaits departure from the new South Shields station on New Year's Eve 2019. The new-style ticket barriers are in evidence. (Colin Alexander)

The original Metro station at South Shields opened in 1984 and handled over 50 million passengers in its thirty-five-year lifetime. This is its replacement, complete with bus interchange facilities, seen on 31 December 2019. (Colin Alexander)

Town Hall of 1910, with its lofty tower. The terminus has relocated twice since the line closed to British Rail services in 1981.

The first South Shields Metro station closed in July 2019 to be replaced by a new £21 million landmark Metro and bus interchange, designed by Harris Partnership.

From South Shields' newest landmark, we could stroll to its oldest, the site of Arbeia Roman fort, then to another new attraction, the National Centre for the Written Word. This stands above the ferry landing from which we could sail across the Tyne to North Shields. Alternatively, we could walk down Ocean Road past the town's excellent museum to the beach and parks, but instead we are going to leap 11 km almost due south to the Metro's Wearside terminus at South Hylton.

Just to the west of the station here is one of the north-east's most famous landmarks, Penshaw Monument. This was built in the style of a Greek Doric temple on top of Penshaw Hill in 1844, in memory of John George Lambton, Earl of Durham. The architects were John Green, builder of the Ouseburn and Willington viaducts, and his son Benjamin who was responsible for the Newcastle and Berwick Railway station at Tynemouth.

Boarding the Metro at South Hylton, which opened in 2002, we may observe the station's colour scheme, designed by artist Morag Morrison. She created the visual identity for most of the Wearside stations, which have a different appearance to those on the 1980s sections.

From south of the Tyne
to south of the Wear.
This is the end of the
line at South Hylton.
Perhaps one day a
westward extension via
the old Leamside line
will connect Sunderland
and Washington
to Pelaw, forming
a loop. Metrocar
No. 4009 stands at
the single platform on
30 December 2019,
having arrived
from the airport.
(Colin Alexander)

Her choice of colours reflects the pale qualities of northern light, and each station has its own unique combination.

We head east, enjoying panoramic views over the Wear valley, looking west to the giant Nissan plant with its associated windfarm, and taking in the new Northern Spire Bridge, opened in 2018. Further east is the massive, green-painted Queen Alexandra Bridge, built by the North Eastern Railway in 1905, and like the High Level Bridge over the Tyne, constructed as a double-decked rail and road bridge. Railway traffic, consisting of coal, ceased as early as 1921. It was designed by Charles Harrison, who was also responsible for the King Edward VII Bridge linking Newcastle and Gateshead.

Pallion, our first stop, was once well-known to railway enthusiasts for its crane tank engines, employed at the former Doxford's shipyard.

We call at the new stations at Millfield and University before arriving at Park Lane interchange, with its attractive blue and green colour scheme. Our train descends a curve past the site of Fawcett Street sidings, and the Durham Coast Line from Teesside and Hartlepool emerges from a tunnel to join us from the right. Mowbray Park, with its graceful war memorial, museum and winter gardens, is opposite as we enter Sunderland station.

Formerly known as Sunderland Central, it opened in 1879 and once boasted a Gothic clock tower and an arched overall roof. Following bomb damage in World War II, its post-war

University is one of the new stations on the South Hylton extension, where 4005 and 4038 are on their way to the airport, in 2014. Some of the buildings of Sunderland University's campus are visible on the right. (Alex Thorkildsen)

Park Lane is a major interchange for local bus services around Sunderland. Metrocars Nos 4067 and 4021 approach the station from the direction of South Hylton on 13 May 2014. (Alex Thorkildsen)

The same Metrocar pairing on the same date pass Fawcett Street sidings as they leave Sunderland for South Hylton. Sunderland station is under the bridge, below the brick building with the five porthole windows. The Durham Coast Line to Hartlepool and Teesside goes off to the right. (Alex Thorkildsen)

Echoing what happened to Tyneside's suburban stations a couple of decades earlier, Sunderland station underwent a major transformation with the arrival of the Metro. Beside Metrocars Nos 4048 and 4028, on a South Hylton to Airport service on 12 February 2014 can be seen some of the 10,000 illuminated glass bricks which form Jason Bruges Studio's 'Platform 5' artwork. (Alex Thorkildsen)

reconstruction was unimaginative and by the 1980s, it was one of the most depressing stations anywhere in the country.

The rebuilding associated with the arrival of Metro services in 2002 saw some revitalisation, as well as rationalisation down to just two platforms. Among the artworks here is 'Platform 5', an ambitious light installation running the length of the station, by Jason Bruges Studio. Echoing Sunderland's industrial heritage, it consists of thousands of glass bricks, which are brought to life by low-energy LEDs which create a constantly changing animation of walking passengers.

Tunnelling beneath Sunderland, with the old circular ventilation shafts above us, we emerge above the River Wear on Thomas Harrison's Monkwearmouth Bridge, which opened in 1879. Alongside it, to the east we cannot miss the Wearmouth Bridge, a 1920s contemporary of the Tyne Bridge. Beyond the road bridge the Wear passes the National Glass Centre then enters the sea.

We will share the rails with 'full-size' passenger and freight trains as far as Pelaw. The modernity of St Peters station contrasts not only with the nearby Anglo-Saxon church of that name, but also its predecessor, the adjacent Grade II* listed Monkwearmouth station. This is another of the fascinating Victorian stations that can be viewed from the Metro. With its handsome Ionic portico, it opened in 1848 as the terminus of the Brandling Junction Railway.

The Wearmouth bridges form one of the more dramatic locations on the Metro system, and just like the Tyne crossing, the transition from tunnel to lofty bridge is a short one. Nos 4003 and 4068 cross the Wear with a train from the airport to South Hylton on 23 October 2013. The North Sea is visible on the right. (Alex Thorkildsen)

St Peters replaced the old Monkwearmouth station on the north bank of the River Wear. Its proximity to the Wearmouth bridges is clear as Nos 4024 and 4059 stop off on their way to South Hylton from Newcastle Airport on 30 December 2019. (Colin Alexander)

Another impressive piece of railway heritage adjacent to the Metro is the 1848 Monkwearmouth station, with its beautiful Ionic portico. The Grade II* listed building was originally the southern terminus of the Brandling Junction Railway and was photographed on 30 December 2019. (Colin Alexander)

Until recently, the station building housed a small railway museum. The new Metro edifice features another illuminated glass-block light installation, this time embedded in the surface of the platforms themselves. This is 'White Light' by Ron Haselden.

The new station at Stadium of Light, of course, serves Sunderland AFC's 'new' ground, which is clearly visible from the train. It was built on the site of Wearmouth Colliery in 1997. Naturally, the station features red and white panelling and the football club's insignia. The next stop, Seaburn, opened in 1937 and was previously the place to alight for Sunderland matches, as it was the closest to the former Roker Park. A walk of less than a mile brings you to the seafront promenade at Roker.

Looking north as we head back towards Tyneside, the 100-foot Cleadon Water Tower and the nearby windmill dominate the skyline. We then come to East Boldon station, which opened as Cleadon Lane in 1839. The level crossing here is protected by automatic barriers, as are the two that follow at Tile Shed Lane and Boldon Lane.

Brockley Whins station opened in 1844 and was, from 1925 until 1991, known as Boldon Colliery. The location was once well known to railway enthusiasts and photographers for Pontop flat crossing, where mineral trains crossed the Durham Coast Line on the level. The bridge that once carried the Stanhope & Tyne line south-westward still stands, and curves trail in east and west of Brockley Whins station leading to the remaining Tyne Dock freight branch. The 2002 station at Fellgate is our last stop before almost 4 kilometres of dead-straight track, mostly between open fields, as we return to Pelaw.

From Pelaw as far as South Gosforth we retrace in reverse the route we took to South Shields. Once out of the shadows of South Gosforth's control centre our South Hylton to Airport service climbs the westbound curve on the former NER 1905 Ponteland branch, giving us a good view of the west end of the car-sheds, where we pass the carriage-washing plant.

East Boldon was one of the existing BR stations on the Newcastle to Sunderland line, and it was upgraded for Metro operation in 2002. Nos 4083 and 4085 are heading to South Hylton on a sunny 27 April 2014. The level crossing here is protected by automatic barriers. (Alex Thorkildsen)

The station at Brockley Whins was known as Boldon Colliery from 1925 to 1991 when it reverted to its original name. The freight line to Tyne Dock curves away to the right as Nos 4003 and 4026 depart for Sunderland and South Hylton on 10 February 2014. (Alex Thorkildsen)

Travelling between Sunderland and Gateshead Stadium, there is a good chance that your Metro train will pass a 'main-line' service. A southbound Grand Central 'HST' of similar vintage to the Metro fleet thunders past Metrocars Nos 4027 and 4080 at Fellgate on 29 June 2012. Note the difference in height between the two trains. (Alex Thorkildsen)

From Pelaw to South Gosforth we retrace in reverse the route we took earlier to South Shields, so we now skip to South Gosforth. Nos 4021 and 4050 are coasting into the station from the Airport branch as they head for Pelaw on 23 October 2013. The line through Benton to the coast curves right and the car sheds are directly ahead of us beyond the trees. (Alex Thorkildsen)

Further around the curve, passengers have a view of Gosforth depot's west yard. Nos 4002 and 4043 are working a train from South Hylton to the airport on 11 March 2014. (Alex Thorkildsen)

This line once continued beyond Ponteland, where reversal was necessary for steam 'autocars' to Darras Hall and mineral trains on their way to and from Kirkheaton Colliery in the Northumberland countryside. Ponteland and Darras Hall lost their passenger services in 1929, although goods traffic continued to use parts of the line to Callerton and Fawdon until the 1980s, carrying explosives and confectionery, respectively. As David Thornton puts it, "gelignite and jelly tots"!

Metro's first stop after leaving South Gosforth is Regent Centre, on the site of the short-lived Edwardian West Gosforth station. Situated next to the old A1 Great North Road, Regent Centre is another of the purpose-built bus interchanges, featuring Anthony Lowe's tiled 'Metro Morning' mural on the outside. Next is Wansbeck Road station, then Fawdon, on the site of the former Coxlodge station. Here we encounter the first of four level crossings on the Airport branch, over each of which trains are restricted to 15 km/h.

We cross the busy A1 Western Bypass before arriving at Kingston Park station, which dates from 1985. Two years before the station opened, a Metro service collided with a double-decker bus on the level crossing at Brunton Lane. The bus driver had ignored the flashing lights, but fortunately, the vehicle was empty and there were no casualties.

Bank Foot is the next station, and this was the terminus of Metro's green line from 1981 to 1991. From here to Callerton Parkway we are in open countryside, and before long we pass the runway lights outside the airport, where we reach the terminal building just twenty-three minutes after leaving the city centre.

It is quite rare to see a single Metrocar in operation. This is Fawdon station and No. 4044 is out on her own in the snow to 'bed in' some new brakes on 29 December 2013. (Alex Thorkildsen)

Pedestrians wait by the level crossing at Kingston Park, once the scene of that altercation between Metro and bus. Nos 4016 and 4048 form a South Hylton to Airport service on 14 June 2014. (Alex Thorkildsen)

Not often seen by the public, a Nexus Rail self-propelled ballast-tamping machine is seen in action at Bank Foot on 13 October 2013. (Alex Thorkildsen)

Celebrity pair Nos 4001 and 4002 approach Bank Foot with a working from the airport to South Hylton on 9 February 2015. (Alex Thorkildsen)

One of Nexus Rail's road-rail vehicles is captured on camera at Callerton Parkway on 22 August 2013. This one is a specially adapted Ford Ranger pick-up. (Alex Thorkildsen)

Metrocar No. 4047 is pictured at the airport awaiting departure for South Hylton, while a Boeing 777 of Emirates Airlines comes in to land from Dubai on 21 September 2012. (Trevor Hall)

8

Metro Future

The plan to extend Metro to Wearside, which eventually came to fruition in 2002, was mentioned in the Test Centre leaflet, printed in the 1970s. The original total of forty-two stations has now become sixty, but more could follow.

Possible future developments include an extension of the line from South Hylton to Washington along an old track-bed, which could then continue north along the former Leamside route to complete a 'Wearside Loop' at Pelaw. A coastal link from South Shields through Sunderland to Seaham and Doxford would serve large areas of population previously unconnected to the rail network.

On the existing South Shields line, the route between Pelaw and Bede has limited capacity, having sections of single track with passing loops. This was to accommodate a parallel freight-only line to the oil terminal at Jarrow, but this route is now disused, which would make it possible to provide double track for Metro throughout.

Newcastle's hilly West End is densely populated but has never been served directly by Metro. Part of the original plan included provision at St James for extension to the west. Recently, however, some massive construction projects in this area involving deep foundations would make any future tunnelling difficult and prohibitively expensive. Therefore, a more economical alternative would be the North East Combined Authority's proposal to use part of the former Newcastle to Hexham line from Forth Banks through Elswick and Scotswood to reach the West End.

Another possibility would be strike west using a new Tyne crossing via the Metrocentre and Team Valley, providing improved public transport links to a badly neglected area of population as well as huge retail and business districts. This proposal could extend through the Team Valley to Lamesley where the East Coast Main Line is crossed by the A1, offering the potential of a parkway-style interchange between road, rail and Metro.

Then there is a proposal for a north–south link from Northumberland Park to Percy Main, alongside the former test-track route, serving Cobalt Business Park and Silverlink Retail Park. This would cross Middle Engine Lane where, of course, it all began with Metro testing.

As well as new lines, there have been proposals for further intermediate stations, such as Murton and Killingworth Moor, where new housing developments are in their infancy beside the existing Metro route.

The possibility of opening up the 'avoiding line' past South Gosforth depot has been explored. This would enable direct services between the airport and North Tyneside, and potentially to South East Northumberland in connection with another oft-discussed development. That is the possible connection at Northumberland Park with a reintroduced passenger service on the former Blyth & Tyne route from Newcastle through Seaton Delaval to Ashington. In addition, much of the old track-bed between the airport and Ponteland remains intact, and this is another scheme for possible consideration.

A scene that could be repeated in the future, if one of the proposed extensions becomes a reality. A train for Newbiggin calls at Longbenton station in 1964. The route taken branched off the North Tyne loop at present-day Northumberland Park Metro station, then continued via Seaton Delaval, New Hartley, Newsham, Bedlington and Ashington. Note the electrified third rails, which were removed after 1967. (JC Dean, NERA collection)

Looking as good as new following her 2012 refurbishment, Metrocar No. 4082 waits between duties inside South Gosforth Depot. Notice the illuminated inspection pits between the rails. In her fortieth year of service at the time of writing, it is a matter of time until she and her sisters are replaced by the new Metro fleet. (Alex Thorkildsen)

Forty-five years young at the time of publication, pioneer No. 4001 shows off her refurbished livery inside
South Gosforth depot on 5 August 2018. I hope that when their pantographs are lowered for the last time, one
of these stalwarts is saved for posterity. (Scott Lowes)

Most importantly, it is intended to introduce a new fleet to replace the original refurbished fleet of eighty-eight Metrocars plus the two prototypes, which have served the people of Tyneside and Wearside since 1980 on the busiest light-rail system outside the capital. They were designed to last for thirty years and the fact that they have exceeded that by 33 per cent is testimony to their sound design and Metro's excellent maintenance engineers.

Replacement is essential, especially as all passenger-number forecasts predict Metro usage will increase. A survey was carried out among Metro passengers in 2012 to seek their opinions on desirable features for the new fleet, in which the general feeling was that they simply wanted newer versions of the same trains, with similar seating and door arrangements.

There is a possibility of the new trains being dual voltage, which would allow them to operate on the 25kv AC system used on the national network, as well as the 1500v DC installed on the

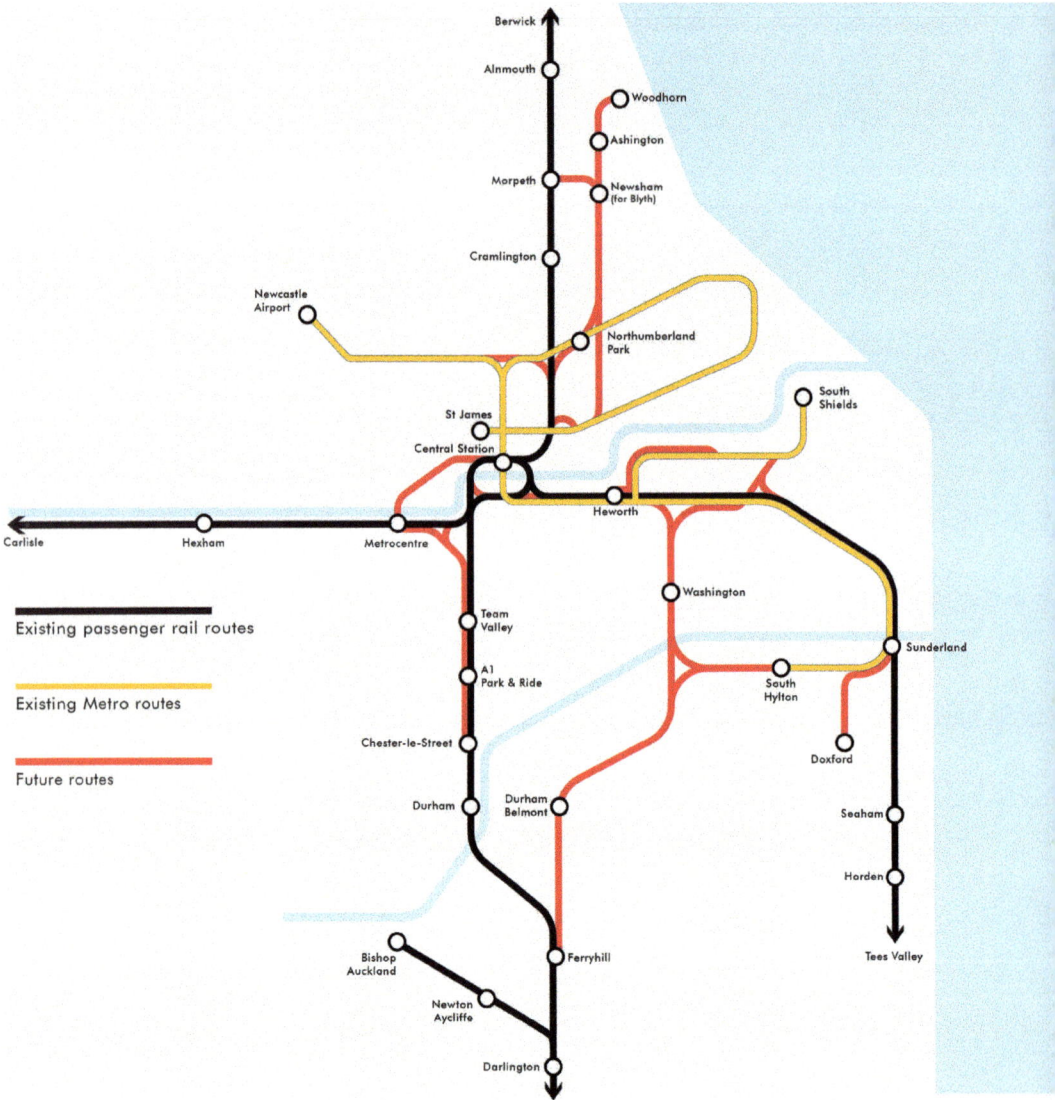

Metro Futures map showing some of the possible extensions to the system and how they fit in with the existing Metro and main line network. (Image courtesy of Nexus)

Metro, increasing flexibility. It is hoped that the trains could be delivered as early as 2021, with construction taking place in either Spain, Switzerland or Newton Aycliffe in County Durham. The last option would be preferable, securing jobs in the north-east at a factory adjacent to George Stephenson's 1825 Stockton & Darlington Railway.

With stations being refurbished and trains being replaced, there is one other major part of Metro's infrastructure in desperate need of updating, and that is South Gosforth depot. At the time of writing, a temporary depot is being built on a former landfill site between Percy Main and Howdon, between the Metro route and the old Riverside branch track-bed. It will be used to maintain a proportion of the current fleet while Gosforth depot is rebuilt in stages and will also be the railhead for delivery by road of the next generation of Metro trains. One possible obstacle to the rebuilding of the old depot is the presence of an asbestos-laden BR DMU vehicle supposedly buried below the ballast at the east end of the sheds!

It is hard to believe that our Metro has kept Tyneside and Wearside moving for forty years, and finally, it is almost time to retire the old faithful Metrocar supertrams. Hopefully at least one will be preserved for posterity. The new trains, when delivered, will bring a new lease of life to the system and hopefully break new ground as extensions are built, bringing all of the benefits of the Metro to previously unconnected parts of Tyneside and Wearside.

This is a 2015 artist's impression of the proposed new Metro train to take us into the 2020s and beyond. Aesthetically, it is not dissimilar to the originals, illustrating the timeless nature of their design. (Image courtesy of Nexus)

Bibliography

Metro Test Centre, leaflet, Tyne & Wear Passenger Transport Executive, mid-1970s.

Tyne & Wear Metro, special supplement, *Financial Times* (4 February 1977).

Meet Your Metro, Tyne & Wear Passenger Transport Executive, July 1977.

Horse Tram to Metro: One Hundred Years of Local Public Transport in Tyne and Wear, Tyne & Wear Passenger Transport Executive, 1978.

Young, Alan, *Suburban Railways of Tyneside* (published by Martin Bairstow, 1999).

'The Beauty of Transport', blog by Daniel Wright.

Nexus website, 'Art on Transport'; www.nexus.org.uk/art/list.

Metro & Local Rail Strategy, draft document, North East Combined Authority & Nexus.

Metro Futures, brochure, North East Combined Authority.